The Holiday Table

· ·

BASED ON THE PUBLIC TELEVISION SERIES

KitchenAid®
FOR THE WAY IT'S MADE.

ISBN 0-9705973-7-1

Printed in Korea

10 9 8 7 6 5 4 3 2 1

MPP Books
363 14th Avenue, San Francisco, California 94118

The Holiday Table

BASED ON THE PUBLIC TELEVISION SERIES

Produced by Marjorie Poore Productions
Photography by Alec Fatalevich

Table of Contents

Introduction

For many people, holiday memories are forever entwined with memories of good food. It all starts at Halloween—one of the few times parents abandon sugar quotas for their kids—with magical memories of collecting countless bags of candy. Thanksgiving brings the unbeatable combination of a perfectly roasted turkey with all the fixings. And don't forget the all-you-can-eat Thanksgiving dessert buffet laden with pies—pumpkin, chocolate, or maybe a luscious banana cream. As the winter holidays approach, visions of creamy mugs of eggnog and buttery rich holiday cookies dance in our heads. Along with family and friends, food also becomes a revered and welcome guest at the holiday table.

While we all have cherished recipes that we make year after year, there are plenty of adventurous cooks out there eager to experiment with a new recipe or ingredient and are ready to start a few new traditions of their own. This quickly became apparent to our *Holiday Table* production staff when our phones started ringing and our inboxes flooded with emails—all asking for holiday-related recipes. This led us to produce an entire series devoted to holiday cooking, featuring recipes from Halloween all the way through to New Year's Day. Our sponsor, KitchenAid, recognized the possibilities immediately and quickly came on board.

This cookbook is a compilation of many of the recipes featured on our holiday programs. Adult Halloween parties were hot so we devoted a number of episodes to spooky and whimsical treats that you'll find here like Bat Wings, Bloody Mary Soup and Witches Fingers, the ultimate "finger" food.

Thanksgiving was always the most popular holiday to our viewers and our hosts—Dede Wilson, Emily Luchetti, and Chris Fennimore—came up with a dazzling array of side dishes, entrees, and desserts, plus a selection of terrific recipes that give new life to those beloved Thanksgiving leftovers.

For the big wave of holidays that occur in December, there was no shortage of recipe ideas. Our favorite topic was "gifts from the kitchen," filled with creative ideas and delicious, inexpensive ways to say "Happy Holidays!" to those you love most. From homemade spiced nuts, cookies, and candy, to marinated olives and cheddar cheese balls, there's a gift for everyone on your list.

Another area that captured our imagination was holiday cookie-making, and the recipes here offer an endless source of inspiration with different shapes, colors, and flavors that create instant holiday magic. Chanukah and Kwaanza gave us a chance to include some wonderful ethnic recipes from guest experts Joyce White, a leading African-American cookbook author, and Mitchell Davis, who brought us some of the best that Jewish cooking has to offer. As the holiday season winds down, you can ring in the New Year with an assortment of enticing brunch recipes, a favorite meal among our various collaborators.

Let the *Holiday Table* make your days merry and bright as you celebrate new traditions with your family and friends.

Halloween

Deviled Eyeballs

MAKES 12 APPETIZERS *Here's an appetizer that will really turn heads on Halloween. To prevent the eggs from rolling around on your serving plate, slice a very small piece off the bottom of the egg white half to create a flat surface on which the egg can sit.*

1 green onion

6 hard-boiled eggs

2 tablespoons mayonnaise

1½ teaspoons Dijon mustard

2 tablespoons chopped parsley

Salt

Ground black pepper

Paprika

6 green or black olives, halved

Slice the white part of the green onion very thinly and set aside. Shell the hard-boiled eggs, the slice them in half horizontally and scoop out the yolks. In a small bowl, mash the yolks with a fork, then add the mayonnaise and mustard. Stir in the reserved green onion and the parsley. Add salt, pepper, and paprika to taste. Using a teaspoon, fill the egg white halves with the egg yolk mixture. Place an olive half on the top of each egg half to resemble eyeballs. Arrange on a platter and serve.

Spicy Bat Wings

SERVES 5 *On All Hallows Eve, everyday chicken wings masquerade as bat wings and come to life with a sweet and spicy barbecue sauce that oozes with flavor.*

20 small chicken wings, tips removed

1 cup ketchup

¼ cup molasses

2 tablespoon minced garlic

1 tablespoon minced ginger

1 bay leaf

2 tablespoon Worcestershire sauce

3 tablespoons cider vinegar

2 tablespoon brown sugar

1 teaspoon salt

1 tablespoon black pepper

2 tablespoon red wine or dark beer

2 tablespoon dry mustard

1 tablespoon Tabasco or dried chili flakes

4 tablespoon chopped cilantro leaves

Preheat oven to 350°F. Bake the chicken wings until they are just cooked, about 20 minutes. Set aside to cool.

While the chicken is baking, combine the rest of the ingredients in a KitchenAid blender and purée until smooth. Pour the mixture into a medium non-reactive pot and bring to a boil. Reduce the heat and allow it to simmer for about 10 minutes.

Put the chicken wings in a large bowl and pour the hot mixture over them. Coat the wings well. On a parchment paper lined baking sheet, arrange the wings in a single layer. Bake for 7 to 10 minutes, or until the wings are heated all the way through.

Transfer the wings to a serving platter, sprinkle with the cilantro and serve.

Goblin Juice

SERVES 4 *The combination of pumpkin purée and apple juice along with fragrant spices makes this a terrific fall treat that will delight kids and adults alike. If using canned pumpkin, make sure it is pure pumpkin purée and not pumpkin pie mix.*

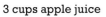

3 cups apple juice

1 small piece fresh ginger

1 cinnamon stick

3 cloves

2 tablespoons honey

2 cups pumpkin purée (see Note)

Pour the apple juice into a saucepan and bring to a simmer over medium-high heat. Add the ginger, cinnamon stick, and cloves and simmer for an additional five minutes. Stir in the honey and set aside to cool. Refrigerate for at least one day or up to 3 days.

Strain the mixture through a fine mesh strainer.

In a KitchenAid food processor or blender, combine one cup of the strained apple juice mixture with the two cups pumpkin purée. Process for 30 seconds. Pour into a fine mesh strainer or china cap to remove pulp. Press down to get out as much liquid as possible. Pour the apple pumpkin mixture back into the apple juice mixture and chill well. Serve cold.

Toasted Pumpkin Seeds

MAKES 1 CUP *Save the seeds from your Jack-O-Lantern. They'll make a tasty and healthy snack by just adding a few spices and toasting them for a few minutes in the oven.*

Basic recipe:

1 cup raw pumpkin seeds

1 tablespoon olive oil

Sea or Kosher Salt

Variations:

Curry powder

Chili powder

Garlic powder

Preheat oven to 375°F.

In a medium bowl, mix together the seeds and olive oil, coating the seeds well. Toss with the salt.

Line a baking sheet with parchment paper or aluminum foil. Spread out the seeds in a single layer on the baking sheet and bake until toasted, about 10 minutes.

For alternative flavor combinations, toss in approximately 1 teaspoon of one of the variation spices along with the salt.

Pumpkin Ragu
with Shell Pasta and Ricotta

SERVES 8 *This is a heartwarming dish that welcomes in the fall. It's important to buy the cooking variety of pumpkin for this recipe, but if you can't find one, substitute butternut squash which is always readily available and tastes just as good.*

24 extra-large pasta shells

1 pumpkin, approximately 4 pounds
   (or the same amount of butternut squash)

2 small onions, sliced

2-inch piece of ginger, grated

1 tablespoon minced garlic

4 tablespoons olive oil

1 red pepper, cut into ½-inch pieces

1 green pepper, cut into ½-inch pieces

8 ounces mushrooms, stems removed and sliced

14 ounces diced tomatoes, canned

¼ cup vegetable or chicken stock

½ cup ricotta cheese

¼ cup fresh chopped basil

½ cup parmesan cheese

Salt

Pepper

Preheat oven to 350°F.

In a large pot of salted water, cook the pasta shells until just tender. Remove from the water, let cool, and lightly toss with oil.

Cut the top off the pumpkin, peel, and remove the seeds. Chop the pumpkin flesh into ½-inch pieces. You will want to end up with approximately 8 cups of chopped pumpkin flesh.

In a large sauté pan, gently fry the onions, ginger, garlic and pumpkin in the olive oil for about 10 minutes, stirring occasionally. Add the red and green peppers and mushrooms and cook for 3 more minutes. Stir in the tomato and stock. Bring to a boil, reduce heat, and simmer until pumpkin is just tender, 15 to 20 minutes. Reserve ½ cup of the mixture and set aside. Stir the ricotta and basil into the bulk of the tomato mixture.

Remove from the heat and spoon the mixture into each of the cooked pasta shells. Spread reserved mixture in the bottom of a lightly oiled casserole dish large enough to hold pasta shells in a single layer. Place the filled pasta shells open side up into the casserole dish. Sprinkle with the parmesan cheese and season with salt and pepper to taste. Cover the casserole and bake for approximately 15 minutes until the pasta shells are completely warmed and the parmesan is melted.

Witches Hair Pasta

SERVES 6 *This dramatic and o-so-scary recipe consists of making orange and black fettuccine or spaghetti from scratch to create Medusa-like "hair". Toss the two colors together with a browned butter-cranberry-pumpkin seed sauce.*

Black Pasta Dough

2¼ cup all-purpose flour

½ teaspoon salt

3 large eggs

2 teaspoons squid ink (see Note)

1 teaspoon olive oil

Orange Pasta Dough

2¼ cup all-purpose flour

½ teaspoon salt

3 large eggs

1 tablespoon annatto powder

1 teaspoon olive oil

Brown Butter Sage Sauce with Pumpkin Seeds and Cranberries (recipe follows)

TO MAKE THE BLACK PASTA DOUGH: Combine flour and salt together in the bowl of a KitchenAid mixer. In a small bowl, whisk together the eggs, squid ink and olive oil. Set the stand mixer on speed 2 (low speed) and slowly pour the egg mixture into the dry ingredients for approximately 2 minutes. Change to a dough hook and knead the dough for 2 to 3 minutes, until the dough is smooth and elastic. If the dough is too dry to form a ball, add 1 tablespoon of cold water. If the dough is sticky, add more flour.

Turn the dough out onto a lightly floured surface and shape the dough into a ball. Transfer the dough to a bowl, cover with plastic wrap, and let rest for at least 25 minutes or up to 2 hours to relax the dough.

TO MAKE THE ORANGE PASTA DOUGH: Combine flour and salt together in the bowl of a KitchenAid mixer. In a small bowl, whisk together the eggs, annatto powder and olive oil. Set the stand mixer on speed 2 (low speed) and slowly pour the egg mixture into the dry ingredients for approximately 2 minutes. Change to a dough hook and knead the dough for 2 to 3 minutes, until the dough is smooth and elastic. If the dough is too dry to form a ball, add 1 tablespoon of cold water. If the dough is sticky, add more flour.

Turn the dough out onto a lightly floured surface and shape the dough into a ball. Transfer the dough to a bowl, cover with plastic wrap, and let rest for at least 25 minutes or up to 2 hours to relax the dough.

TO ROLL AND SHAPE THE PASTA: Cut the pasta dough into pieces about ⅜-inch thick. Flatten each piece slightly and set aside.

Attach the pasta sheet roller to the KitchenAid mixer. Set adjustment knob on the Pasta Sheet Roller at 1.

Turn the mixer to speed 2 or 4. Feed a flattened piece of dough through the rollers to knead. Fold the dough in half and roll again. Repeat this several times, until dough is smooth and pliable. Lightly dust the pasta with flour while rolling and cutting to help it dry quicker and keep it from sticking together. Set the pasta sheet aside and repeat with the rest of the pieces of dough.

Move the adjustment knob to number 2. Feed the dough through the rollers to further flatten it. Change the setting to 3 and feed dough through the rollers again. Continue to increase the roller setting until the desired dough thickness is reached.

To make fettuccine or spaghetti, detach the pasta sheet roller and attach the pasta cutter attachment. Feed the flattened sheets of dough through the cutter. You can use the cut pasta immediately or you can freeze or dry the pasta for later.

TO COOK THE FRESH PASTA: Bring a large pot of salted water to a rolling boil. Add the pasta and cook for 2 to 3 minutes until al dente. Remember that fresh pasta cooks much quicker than dry pasta. Be careful not to overcook or it will become mushy.

NOTE: *If you can't find it locally, squid ink can be purchased from suppliers on the internet.*

Brown Butter Sage Sauce with Pumpkin Seeds and Cranberries

8 tablespoons butter (1 stick)

3 sage leaves, sliced thinly

1 cup dried cranberries

1 cup pepito seeds (shelled pumpkin seeds)

Melt the butter in a large sauté pan. Let the butter cook on medium-high heat until lightly browned and it gives off a nutty aroma. Add the sage leaves and stir to coat the leaves. Add the cranberries and continue stirring for 30 seconds, then add the pepito seeds. Toss and coat well and continue cooking for another 30 seconds. Serve immediately over the black and orange pasta.

Bloody Mary Soup

SERVES 4 *Here's a fun soup which remains true to its namesake except for the alcohol. It comes together in a very short time and is the perfect first course to serve after a hard night of trick or treating.*

2 tablespoons butter

1 medium onion, finely chopped

1 clove minced garlic

1 stalk celery, finely chopped

1 tablespoon sugar

½ teaspoon celery seed

One 28-ounce can Italian plum tomatoes

1 tablespoon Worcestershire sauce

Juice of one lemon

Salt

Pepper

Tabasco sauce

Celery leaves for garnish

Chopped fresh parsley for garnish

Melt the butter in a three-quart saucepan over medium heat. Add the onions, garlic, and celery and sweat until soft and translucent, about 3 minutes.

Add the sugar, celery seed and tomatoes (including the juices). Bring to a boil and simmer for 5 minutes. Using a KitchenAid immersion blender, purée until smooth.

Season the soup with the Worcestershire sauce, lemon juice, salt, pepper, and Tabasco to taste.

Ladle into bowls and garnish with celery leaves and fresh parsley.

Dracula Nori Rolls

MAKES 24 PIECES *With a delicious, Asian-flavored shrimp filling rolled in Nori (Japanese seaweed), this bite-sized appetizer adds sophistication to any Halloween gathering. If you can't find Kaffir lime leaves, try substituting a small amount of lime zest.*

1 pound raw shrimp

1½ tablespoons fish sauce

1 tablespoon sake

2 tablespoon cilantro

1 Kaffir lime leaf, shredded (optional)

1 tablespoon lime juice

2 tablespoon sweet chili sauce

1 egg white, lightly beaten

5 sheets Nori (Japanese seaweed sheets)

Dipping Sauce

⅓ cup sweet chili sauce

1 tablespoon lime juice

Using a Kitchenaid food processor with a multipurpose blade, pulse the shrimp, fish sauce, sake, cilantro, lime leaf, lime juice, and chili sauce until smooth. Add the egg whites and mix well.

Spread the mixture over a sheet of nori, leaving a ½-inch border. Roll tightly, cover, and refrigerate for 1 hour.

When well chilled, trim each end then cut the roll into ¾-inch pieces. Place into a bamboo steamer and steam for 5 minutes, or until cooked through.

For the dipping sauce, whisk together the chili sauce and lime juice in a small bowl.

Arrange the rolls on a serving platter and serve with the dipping sauce.

Witches' Fingers

MAKES 5 DOZEN *You'll be amazed how these cookies really look like old crooked witches' fingers with their nails of blanched almonds. They are easy to make and sure to cause a commotion among kids and adults alike.*

1 cup butter, softened

1 cup powdered sugar

1 egg

1 teaspoon almond extract

1 teaspoon vanilla extract

2⅔ cup flour

1 teaspoon baking powder

1 teaspoon salt

¾ cup whole blanched almonds

1 tube red decoration gel (optional)

Preheat oven to 350°F.

In the bowl of a KitchenAid stand mixer, beat together the butter, sugar, egg, almond and vanilla extracts. Lowering the speed, add in the flour, baking powder, and salt, beating just until the dry ingredients are combined.

Cover and refrigerate for 30 minutes. Working with one quarter of the dough at a time, and keeping the remainder in the refrigerator, roll a heaping teaspoon of dough into a finger shape for each cookie. Press one almond firmly into one end for the nail. Squeeze the centre to form the knuckle shape. Using a paring knife, make slashes on top of the cookie for the knuckle. Using the back of the knife, create a straight edge at the opposite end of the nail side of the finger to make it look as if the finger was cut from the hand.

Place on a parchment paper–lined baking sheet and bake for 20 to 25 minutes, or until pale golden.

Note: To create a blood effect under the "nail,", after baking remove the almond "nail" and spread the red gel in the nail area. Then reapply the almond "nail".

Spider Web Cupcakes

Excerpted from *A Baker's Field Guide to Cupcakes*, by Dede Wilson. © 2006, used by permission from The Harvard Common Press.

MAKES 18 CUPCAKES *The clever spiderweb pattern on the icing makes these perfect for Halloween. It's easy to make the spider web. Just pipe on melted white chocolate in a spiral and draw a knife blade through the spiral. Everyone will think you bought them at a bakery.*

Chocolate Cupcakes

1½ cups all-purpose flour

½ cup Dutch-processed cocoa powder

¾ teaspoon baking soda

¼ teaspoon salt

½ cup (1 stick) unsalted butter, at room temperature, cut into small pieces

1⅓ cups sugar

1 teaspoon vanilla extract

2 large eggs

1 cup milk, at room temperature

Ganache Glaze and Frosting

1 cup whipping cream

15 ounces semisweet or bittersweet chocolate, finely chopped

6 ounces white chocolate, melted

Quart size sealable plastic bags

Preheat oven to 350°F. Line muffin tins for 18 cupcakes with cupcake liners.

TO MAKE THE CUPCAKES: In a bowl, whisk together the flour, cocoa powder, baking soda, and salt to aerate and combine. In a KitchenAid stand mixer with the paddle attachment, beat the butter until creamy, approximately 2 minutes. Add sugar gradually, beating until light and fluffy, about 3 minutes, scraping down the bowl once or twice. Beat in the vanilla extract. Beat in the eggs one at a time, scraping down the bowl after each addition. Add the flour mixture in 4 additions, alternating with the milk. Begin and end with the flour mixture, and beat briefly until smooth on low-medium speed after each addition.

Divide batter evenly among the cupcake wells. Bake for about 22 minutes, or until a toothpick inserted in the center shows a few moist crumbs.

Let cool on wire racks for 5 minutes, then transfer each cupcake to a wire rack to cool completely.

TO MAKE THE GANACHE: In a medium-large saucepan bring the cream to a boil over medium heat.

Remove from the heat and immediately sprinkle the chocolate into the cream. Cover and allow it to sit for 5 minutes. The heat of the cream should melt the chocolate. Gently stir the ganache until smooth.

Use a small offset spatula to apply ganache generously and smoothly to the top of each cupcake.

TO CREATE THE SPIDER WEB PATTERN: Be sure the Ganache is still in a fluid state on the cupcakes.

Spoon the melted white chocolate into a small sealable plastic bag. Snip a very small opening in the bag for piping. Starting at the center of a cupcake, pipe a spiral of white chocolate on the cupcake. Be sure to squeeze gently and pipe the spiral all the way to the outer edge of the cupcake (about 4 spirals). While the Ganache and the white chocolate are still soft, again starting at the center, draw the tip of a thin sharp knife toward the edge of the cupcake. Repeat this in a spoke pattern (about 6 spokes) to create a spiderweb pattern. Chill the cupcakes briefly until the glaze is set. Arrange on a platter and serve.

Notes: The key to making successful "spiderwebs" is to have the ganache glaze and the melted white chocolate both in a fluid state so that when you draw your knife through them, they pull into attractive shapes.

Black and Orange Ice Cream Cake

SERVES 8 TO 12 *Here's a delicious dessert with luscious pumpkin ice cream sandwiched between two layers of moist, rich chocolate cake. It's topped off with spoonfuls of drippy caramel sauce. If you are rushed for time, high-quality caramel sauce from the supermarket will taste great too.*

1 cup sugar

1 cup flour

¾ cup cocoa powder

1 teaspoon baking soda

½ teaspoon baking powder

¼ teaspoon kosher salt

2 large eggs

½ cup buttermilk

4 tablespoons unsalted butter, melted

½ cup coffee

1.75 quart container store bought or homemade pumpkin ice cream, slightly softened

1½ cups caramel sauce (see page 140)

Preheat the oven to 350°F.

Grease and flour the bottom and sides of a 9-inch spring form pan. Sift together the sugar, flour, cocoa powder, baking soda and baking powder. Add the salt. In the bowl of a KitchenAid stand mixer, beat together the eggs and the buttermilk. With the mixer running, add in the melted butter and the coffee. Slowly add the dry ingredients, beating just until combined. Spread in the pan and bake until a skewer inserted in the middle comes out clean, about 25 minutes.

Cool the cake completely and remove it from the spring form pan. Slice off the top of the cake so it is flat on top. Cut the cake in half horizontally. Place the top half of the cake back into the spring form pan. Spread the ice cream on top. Place the second cake layer on top, bottom side up, pressing the cake gently so it sticks to the ice cream. Freeze for at least one hour until the ice cream is firm. Unmold the cake by removing the ring.

To serve, pour caramel sauce over the top of the cake. Cut into pieces.

Note: If the caramel sauce is too cold to pour, warm it. If it is too hot it will run off the cake.

Quick Pumpkin Nut Bread

SERVES 16 *Fragrant and moist, this quick bread comes together in minutes and is great to have around for snacks or unexpected guests. Try making it in muffin tins or miniature cake pans too. Just be sure to adjust the cooking time to compensate for the smaller size.*

- 3½ cups flour
- 1½ teaspoons baking powder
- 1 teaspoon baking soda
- 1½ teaspoons salt
- 1½ teaspoons nutmeg
- 2 teaspoons cinnamon
- 4 eggs
- 3 cups sugar
- 2 cups canned pumpkin
- ⅔ cup water
- 1 cup vegetable oil
- 2 teaspoons vanilla extract
- 1 cup chopped toasted walnuts or toasted pecans
- 1 cup blond raisins (optional)

Preheat oven to 350°F. Grease 2 loaf pans.

Whisk the flour, baking powder, baking soda, salt, nutmeg and cinnamon together in a mixing bowl. Combine the eggs and sugar into a KitchenAid stand mixer and beat well. Add the pumpkin, water, oil, and vanilla and beat again. Lower the speed, and add the dry ingredients into the pumpkin mixture beating until just combined. Fold in the nuts and raisins.

Divide the batter evenly between the 2 greased loaf pans. Bake for about one hour or until a toothpick comes out clean.

Thanksgiving

Side Dishes

Patapan Squash, Gingered Baby Carrots, and Pearl Onions

SERVES 4 TO 6 *A slightly sweet, buttery glaze and fresh ginger flavor work well with these tender fall vegetables. Look for real baby carrots, not the bags of mini carrots sold in abundance at all the grocery stores—you'll taste the difference.*

- 2 pounds patapan squash
- 2 pounds whole baby carrots (with green tops still attached)
- 2 tablespoons butter
- 2 tablespoons sugar
- 1 tablespoon minced fresh ginger
- 1 cup pearl onions

Wash and trim the squash and carrots, leaving some of the small green stems on the carrots. In a sauté pan, heat ¼ cup water with 1 tablespoon of the butter and 1 table-spoon of the sugar. Add the squash and cook, covered, for 3 to 4 minutes. Remove the cover and continue to cook over medium high heat until the water is evaporated and the squash is glazed with the sugar and butter. In a second sauté pan, heat ¼ cup water with the remaining 1 tablespoon butter and 1 tablespoon of sugar. Add the baby carrots, ginger, and pearl onions and cook, covered, for 3 to 4 minutes. Remove the cover and cook over medium high heat until the water is evaporated and the carrots and onions are glazed. Combine all the vegetables together and serve.

Roasted Butternut Squash Soup

SERVES 10 *Here's a creamy, rich butternut squash soup that delivers the deep flavor of roasted vegetables. For extra delicious flavor, use homemade chicken broth or stock, which can be made and frozen weeks ahead.*

- 1 large (about 2½ pounds) butternut squash, peeled, seeded and cut into quarters lengthwise
- 1 large onion, cut in half lengthwise
- 2 large cloves garlic, cut into quarters
- 2 tablespoons olive oil
- 5 cups chicken broth
- 1 can (15 ounces) pumpkin purée, divided
- ¾ teaspoon salt
- ¼ teaspoon cayenne pepper
- 1 cup whipping cream

Preheat oven to 450°F. Using the 2 mm slicing disc, process the squash in a KitchenAid food processor. Transfer the squash to a large mixing bowl. Slice the onion in the food processor and add the onion and garlic to the squash. Drizzle with olive oil and toss the vegetables to coat. Spread in 15-by-10-by-1-inch pan. Bake for 30 to 35 minutes until tender, stirring once or twice. Cool slightly.

Using the multipurpose blade, process ½ of the roasted vegetable mixture and their juices, ¾ cup chicken broth, ½ of the pumpkin purée, salt and cayenne pepper until smooth, about 30 seconds. Transfer to a soup pot. Process the remaining vegetables, pumpkin purée, and ¾ cup chicken broth and add to soup pot. Stir in remaining 3½ cups chicken broth.

Cook and stir over medium heat until thoroughly heated. Stir in the cream and heat just until hot. Serve warm.

Roasted Artichoke Hearts

SERVES 8 TO 10 *This delicious appetizer of artichokes roasted with a crunchy topping of breadcrumbs and cheese is simply irresistible. Use frozen artichokes, which are readily available and aren't laden with oil like you often find in the jarred variety.*

> 2 pounds fresh or frozen artichoke hearts, thawed
> Juice of 1 lemon
> 1 cup flour
> 2 tablespoon olive oil
> 2 cups breadcrumbs
> ¼ teaspoon salt
> ¼ teaspoon black pepper
> 1 tablespoon minced parsley
> 1 tablespoon grated Romano cheese
> 2 eggs, beaten

Preheat the oven to 375°F.

Sprinkle the artichokes with the lemon juice. Spoon the flour into a sealable plastic bag and add about ¼ of the artichokes. Seal the bag and shake to coat them in the flour. Remove the artichokes from the bag, shake off the excess flour, and set aside on a plate. Repeat with the remaining artichokes.

Coat a baking sheet with the olive oil. In a bowl, combine the breadcrumbs with the salt, pepper, parsley, and Romano cheese until well mixed. Taking a few artichokes at a time, dip them into the beaten eggs and then coat with the breadcrumbs. Place the breaded artichoke hearts on the baking sheet. Turn them once to coat with the oil.

Bake for 20 minutes, turning them once halfway through the baking. They should be crunchy and brown on both sides.

Brussels Sprouts with Sweet and Sour Bacon Dressing

SERVES 8 *It's amazing how these Brussels sprouts come alive when they are paired with the smoky flavor of bacon and then dressed in a sweet and sour glaze. These will become a Thanksgiving tradition at your house.*

> 2 pounds Brussels sprouts
> ¼ pound bacon
> 2 tablespoons cider vinegar
> 2 tablespoons sugar

Trim the outer leaves of the sprouts and cut a small "X" in the base of each one.

Boil them in salted water for 6 to 10 minutes until crisp-tender. Drain well,

Fry the bacon in a large skillet until crisp. Drain on paper towels and reserve 2 tablespoons of the drippings. Crumble the bacon into small pieces, and set aside.

Sauté the Brussels sprouts in the drippings until they begin to caramelize. Add the vinegar and sugar and continue to cook over medium heat until the sprouts are glazed.

Transfer to a serving dish and sprinkle with the crumbled bacon.

Green Beans with Balsamic Caramelized Red Onions

SERVES 4 TO 6 *Caramelizing onions takes time so you have to be patient, but the rewards are well worth the effort as they transform into a heavenly sweet topping for the green beans. The onions will keep well for several days in the refrigerator, making this an ideal recipe to do ahead of time.*

6 tablespoons olive oil

1½ pounds red onions, sliced thinly

2½ tablespoons balsamic vinegar

1½ tablespoons grenadine, optional

Salt

Pepper

1 pound green beans, trimmed

1 teaspoon fresh thyme

Heat 3 tablespoons of the olive oil in a large pan. Sauté the onions until dark brown, about 30 minutes. Just before the onions are done, pour in 1½ tablespoons of the balsamic vinegar and the grenadine (if using). Continue to sauté until the liquids coat the onions. Season with salt and pepper to taste. Transfer to a large bowl and keep warm.

In a small bowl, whisk the remaining 3 tablespoon of olive oil, 1 tablespoon vinegar, and the thyme and set aside.

Cook the green beans in lightly salted boiling water until just tender. Drain and toss with the onions. Pour the balsamic mixture over the beans and onions, toss to combine, and serve.

Best-Ever Baked Mashed Potatoes

SERVES 6 TO 8 *This new twist on mashed potatoes gives it an Italian flavor. For optimum results, buy high quality cheeses and salami which are available at Italian markets or through the internet at sites such as www.pennmac.com (Pennsylvania Macaroni).*

6 to 7 large potatoes (Russet, Idaho or Yukon Gold)

1 tablespoon salt

8 tablespoons (1 stick) butter

½ cup milk

½ pound mozzarella cheese, cubed

3 tablespoons grated Romano cheese

⅛ pound hard salami, minced

Pepper

½ cup breadcrumbs

Preheat oven to 350°F.

Peel the potatoes and cut into 1-inch chunks. Transfer to a large saucepan and add cold water to cover. Add 1 tablespoon salt and bring to a boil. Cook the potatoes until they are tender, about 10 to 12 minutes, then drain. Mash the potatoes, then add 6 tablespoons of the butter and the milk.

Using a KitchenAid stand mixer, whip the potatoes until smooth. Reduce to low speed, and add the mozzarella, Romano cheese, and the salami and mix until just combined. Add salt and pepper to taste. Use 1 tablespoon of the butter to grease the bottom and sides of a high-sided casserole dish. Coat the bottom and sides with the breadcrumbs. Spoon the potato mixture into the casserole and dot the top with the remaining 1 tablespoon butter. Bake until the top is golden brown, approximately 30 minutes.

Be careful. This dish is VERY hot when it comes out of the oven!

Potato and Camembert Terrine

SERVES 8 TO 10 *Here's an unbeatable combination: potatoes, apples and Camembert cheese, layered together in a terrine that is as attractive as it is delicious. This dish needs to be made the day before, but since it's served at room temperature, it needs no reheating.*

6 new potatoes (unpeeled)

3 green apples

1 tablespoon lemon juice

6 tablespoons butter

3 tablespoons olive oil

6½ ounces Camembert cheese
(chilled and thinly sliced)

2 tablespoons parsley, finely chopped

2 teaspoons kosher salt

2 teaspoons white pepper

Preheat oven to 350°F.

Parboil the potatoes in lightly salted water for about 15 minutes, or until just tender. Drain and cool. When cool enough to handle, peel the potatoes and cut them into ½-inch-thick slices.

Peel and core the apples and then cut into ¼-inch-thick slices. Toss the apples in the lemon juice and set aside.

Heat 4 tablespoons of the butter and 1½ tablespoons of the olive oil and cook the potatoes over medium heat until golden brown. Drain and cool.

Heat the remaining 2 tablespoons of butter and remaining 1½ tablespoons of oil and cook the apples over medium heat until golden brown. Drain and cool.

Line a 5-by-8-inch loaf pan or ceramic dish (the "terrine") with parchment paper. Place a layer of potatoes on the bottom of the terrine. Then add a layer of apples and follow with a layer of cheese slices. Sprinkle with parsley, salt and pepper. Continue layering and finish with potatoes.

Cover the terrine with foil. Place the terrine in a larger baking pan and fill the larger pan with water until it reaches halfway up the side of the terrine. (This is called a "water bath.") Bake for about 30 minutes. Remove from the oven. Fill another terrine pan or loaf pan with water and place it on top of the potato terrine. Let cool, then refrigerate overnight with the weights which will help compact the terrine as it cools. The pan on top of the terrine should not touch the sides of the potato terrine pan. Serve at room temperature, or place in a 300°F oven for 10 to 15 minutes prior to serving, just until warm, but not hot.

Sweet Potato Soufflé

SERVES 6 TO 8 *If the word "soufflé" makes you apprehensive, this recipe will change your mind. It's a fool-proof version that gives sweet potatoes a wonderful, light texture juxtaposed with a crunchy not-too-sweet topping.*

4 to 5 medium sweet potatoes or yams

4 tablespoons butter

1 can evaporated milk

2 tablespoons brown sugar

1 teaspoon salt

2 eggs, separated

Topping

4 tablespoons butter, softened

4 tablespoons brown sugar

1 cup chopped pecans

1 teaspoon cinnamon

Preheat oven to 450°F. Butter a 3- or 4-quart round casserole.

Pierce the skin of each sweet potato several times with a fork. Bake on a foil-lined pan for 1 hour.

Lower the oven temperature to 350°F.

When the potatoes are cool enough to handle, cut them in half and scoop the flesh into a large bowl. Discard the skins. Add the butter, evaporated milk, brown sugar, and salt, and mix well.

Let the mixture cool completely. Beat the egg yolks into the potato mixture.

In the bowl of a KitchenAid stand mixer, using the wire whip, beat the egg whites until they form stiff peaks. Fold them into the potato mixture. Spoon the mixture into the casserole and bake for 30 minutes.

TO MAKE THE TOPPING: In a small bowl mix together the butter, brown sugar, chopped pecans, and the cinnamon. Sprinkle the topping over the top of the potato casserole and bake for another 10 minutes or until a knife inserted near the centre comes out clean. Serve immediately.

Sweet Potato Tarts

MAKES EIGHT 5-INCH TARTS *This classic sweet potato recipe is elevated into an elegant side dish with its unique presentation in tartlet molds, which allows each dinner guest to have their own serving. The technique for roasting yams at high temperature may seem unusual, but rest assured, the results are creamy and delicious.*

2 yams (enough to make 2 cups roasted)

Crust

1 cup flour

½ teaspoon salt

⅓ cup shortening

3 to 4 tablespoons cold water

1 to 2 tablespoons finely ground toasted pecans

Filling

2 eggs plus one egg yolk, lightly beaten

¾ cup sugar

½ teaspoon ginger

½ teaspoon salt

¼ teaspoon cloves

1 cup 2% milk

⅔ cup light cream

2 teaspoons melted butter

Preheat oven to 450°F.

Clean the yams well and pierce them with a fork. Place them on a foil-lined baking sheet and bake until the yams are fork tender, about 1 hour. When cool enough to handle, peel the potatoes.

TO MAKE THE CRUST: In the bowl of a KitchenAid food processor with a multipurpose blade, pulse together the flour, salt, and shortening. Gradually sprinkle in the cold water and continue to pulse until the flour is moistened and the dough pulls away from the side of the bowl. Gather into a ball, flatten into a disk, and refrigerate for 15 minutes.

Divide the dough into 8 pieces. Roll each piece into a ball and then roll out to fit into individual tart pans that are approximately 5 inches in diameter. Sprinkle ground pecans over each tart crust. Place the pans on a baking sheet.

Reduce the oven temperature to 425°F.

TO MAKE THE FILLING: In the bowl of a KitchenAid stand mixer, beat together the eggs and egg yolk, sugar, ginger, salt, cloves, milk, cream, and butter until well blended. Divide the filling evenly among the prepared crusts and bake for 15 minutes. Lower the oven temperature to 350°F. and continue to bake for an additional 40 to 45 minutes, until the filling is set.

Cranberry Tangerine Relish

MAKES ABOUT 4 CUPS *Don't let the simplicity of this cranberry sauce fool you—the combination of tangerines and cranberries makes entirely new flavors everyone will love. If you use fresh cranberries, the natural pectins will create a more solid gel while frozen cranberries result in a looser jelly.*

- 1 cup sugar
- 1 cup water
- 3 tangerines, seeded and chopped (about 1 cup total, see Note)
- 4 cups frozen or fresh cranberries, rinsed (see headnote)

In a saucepan, over medium heat, cook the sugar and water until dissolved. Add the tangerines and the cranberries and bring to a boil. Lower the heat and simmer for another 10 minutes. Pour into a bowl. Let cool and then refrigerate until completely chilled.

Note: If you can't find fresh tangerines, you can substitute with canned mandarin oranges. Drain the oranges before using.

Andouille Sausage Stovetop Stuffing

4 TO 6 SERVINGS *When a stuffing recipe calls for andouille sausage and jalapeños, you know it will spice up your Thanksgiving table. And, because it's made on the stovetop it saves precious oven space for the turkey. It comes from Chicago chef Jimmy Bannos whose famed Heaven on Seven restaurants have been bringing Cajun food to happy Chicago diners for many years.*

- 2 cups diced andouille sausage
- 1 cup diced yellow onion
- 1 cup diced celery
- 2 cups diced green pepper
- 2 jalapeño peppers, finely diced
- 1 tablespoon roasted garlic
- 1 tablespoon Creole seasoning.
- 3 cups chicken stock
- 3½ cups cornbread, cut into 1-inch cubes
- 1 cup shredded parmesan cheese
- 2 tablespoons chopped parsley
- Salt
- Pepper

In a large sauté pan, sauté the andouille sausage until cooked through. Drain the excess fat. Add the onion, celery, green pepper, jalapeños, garlic, and Creole seasoning and stir to combine. Add the chicken stock and bring the mixture to a simmer on low heat for 10 minutes, stirring occasionally. Add the cornbread, cheese, and parsley and continue cooking, stirring frequently, for an additional 5 minutes. Add salt and pepper to taste.

Italian-Style Stuffing

SERVES 8 TO 10 *Here's a delicious Italian twist on stuffing that comes from Tony Mantuano, the Executive Chef of Spiaggia, a world-renowned Italian restaurant in Chicago. He is an award-winning chef and author of* The Spiaggia Cookbook *published by Chronicle Books.*

1 medium sized acorn squash, peeled and diced

2 sticks (8 ounces) butter

15 medium sage leaves, thinly sliced

14 cups fresh Ciabatta bread,
    cut into 1-inch squares

2 cups chicken stock

1 cup slightly crushed amaretti cookies

2 tablespoons stone-ground mustard

1 cup Parmigiano-Reggiano cheese,
    finely grated, plus extra for serving

Sea salt

Freshly ground pepper

Preheat the oven to 325°F.

Place the diced squash in a medium saucepan and add cold water to cover. Bring to a boil over high heat and cook until tender, about 8 to 10 minutes. Drain and set aside.

In a medium sauté pan, over medium-high heat, melt the butter until the foam subsides and the butter turns a nut brown color, about 4 to 5 minutes. Turn off the heat and quickly add the sage leaves, being careful not to splatter.

In a large bowl, combine the diced bread, chicken stock, squash, amaretti cookies, the sage browned butter, mustard, and cheese and mix well to combine. Season to taste with salt and pepper.

Spoon the stuffing into a 3-quart oven-proof pan and bake for 45 minutes, or until golden brown. Remove from the oven and sprinkle with extra Parmigiano-Reggiano cheese. Serve immediately.

Muffin Stuffing

SERVES 10 TO 12 *At first glance this may seem like a typical stuffing, but there are two secrets that really put this recipe over the top. First, the stuffing is baked in individual muffin tins, giving each serving a wonderful crunchy coating. The second is using Challah, a Jewish egg bread that makes a delicious base for the stuffing.*

1 pound bacon, cut into ½-inch pieces

4 tablespoons butter

2 onions, chopped

2 stalks of celery, chopped

1 teaspoon poultry seasoning

1 cup chicken or turkey broth

1 large loaf of day old Challah bread (see note)

Salt

Pepper

Preheat the oven to 400°F. Butter a 12-cup muffin pan.

Place the bacon in a large cold skillet and cook over medium heat until brown. Pour off the fat. Add the butter to the bacon in the skillet and stir to melt. Add the onions and celery and cook until translucent, 5 to 7 minutes. Add the poultry seasoning and broth. Cut the bread into 1-inch cubes and place in a large mixing bowl. Add the bacon-vegetable mixture to the bread and mix well.

Place a large scoop of stuffing into each muffin cup. Bake until the tops and sides are light brown. Can be made ahead and rewarmed just before serving.

Note: any white bread can be substituted if you can't find Challah. For a richer flavor, try brioche.

Entrees

Creole-Spiced Grilled Jerk Turkey Breast

SERVES 4 *This Creole-inspired recipe from Chicago chef Jimmy Bannos from Heaven on Seven restaurants can be roasted in the oven or cooked on the grill. It takes advantage of the great pre-made dry rubs and spices now available in supermarkets, or you can always make your own from scratch.*

2½ pound boneless turkey breast, skin-on

4 teaspoons dry jerk spice

½ tablespoon Creole spice

3 tablespoons wet jerk spice

2 tablespoons olive oil

Rub the turkey breast with the dry jerk spice and the Creole spice. Rub the wet jerk spice into the turkey breast and place it into a resealable plastic bag. Let marinate for two hours in the refrigerator.

Preheat oven to 350°F or set a gas grill on medium heat. Remove the turkey from the plastic bag and drizzle with the olive oil. Place the turkey in a roasting pan or on the grill skin-side down. Cover with foil and cook for 12 minutes. Turn the turkey breast over, and continue to cook, uncovered, for 30 minutes or until a meat thermometer reads 160°F. Let the turkey rest for 10 minutes before slicing.

Note: To create cross-hatch marks on the turkey, let the turkey to cook for 7 minutes on the first side. Then give it a one-quarter turn and allow it to cook another 5 minutes before cooking on the second side.

Cornish Game Hens with Apple Sausage Cornbread Stuffing

SERVES 4 *Try this recipe if you are having fewer guests to dinner this year. With each person getting their own bird, they will feel very special, especially after taking a bite of the cornbread stuffing that is flavored with sausage, apples, and pecans.*

Apple Sausage Cornbread Stuffing

½ pound breakfast sausage

3 tablespoons butter

1 large onion, chopped

1 large Granny Smith apple,
   peeled, cored and chopped

½ teaspoon ground sage or poultry seasoning

1 cup chicken stock

3 cups diced cornbread

½ cup chopped pecans

4 Rock Cornish Game hens (see Note),
   1 to 1½ pounds each, rinsed and
   dried thoroughly

1 lemon

Salt

Pepper

1 stick (8 tablespoons) butter, melted

Preheat the oven to 400°F.

TO MAKE THE CORNBREAD STUFFING: Brown the sausage in a large skillet, breaking the meat into small pieces. Remove from the pan and drain the excess fat. Add the butter and onion to the pan and cook until soft. Add the apples and cook until they begin to soften. Return the sausage to the pan, add the sage, and the chicken stock and, using a wooden spoon, scrape up the flavorful bits from the bottom of the pan. Add the cornbread and pecans and toss until well mixed and moistened.

TO MAKE THE ROCK CORNISH GAME HENS: Rub the outside of each game hen with the lemon and season inside and out with salt and pepper. Fill each bird loosely with ½ cup of the stuffing and secure the legs with twine. Place into a roasting pan, allowing enough room so the birds do not touch one another. Baste with the melted butter and roast for 20 minutes. Reduce heat to 350°F, tent with foil, and continue to roast for 20 minutes. Remove the foil, brush again with butter, and roast until the skin is crispy and the internal temperature is 170°F.

Roast Turkey with Vanilla and Orange Glaze

SERVES 8 TO 10 *Chef Jean-Pierre Brehier, who has a popular cooking school in Fort Lauderdale, shares his favorite turkey recipe with us. The orange and vanilla give the turkey a wonderfully fragrant scent. As a French-trained chef, he calls for a liberal amount of butter on the skin which adds tremendous flavor and makes the turkey brown beautifully.*

One 14-pound turkey

Salt

Black pepper

½ pound (1 cup) butter, at room temperature

1 Granny Smith apple, cored and cut into chunks

1 large onion, cut into chunks

2 large oranges, skin on, cut into chunks

1 celery stalk, cut into chunks

½ cup orange juice concentrate

2 tablespoons honey

1 tablespoon pure vanilla extract

Preheat the oven to 325°F.

Pat the turkey dry with paper towels and season inside and out with salt and pepper. Brush the outside of the turkey with the butter.

Stuff the cavity of the turkey with the apples, onion, oranges, and celery. Tie the legs together with kitchen twine.

Place the turkey, uncovered, in a large roasting pan and roast until a meat thermometer inserted between the body and the leg into the thickest part of the inner thigh registers 160°F. (this will take approximately 3½ hours, but start checking after 3 hours).

Remove the turkey from the oven and let rest.

In a small bowl, mix together the orange juice concentrate, honey, and vanilla extract and brush onto the outside of the turkey. Roast the turkey for another 10 or 15 minutes, or until the internal temperature reaches 165°F.

Remove the turkey from the oven and cover with aluminum foil. Let rest for 30 minutes before carving.

Turkey with Grappa and Gremolata

SERVES 8 TO 10 *Renowned chef Tony Mantuano of Spiagga in Chicago shared with us his favorite turkey recipe, which we found truly extraordinary with Italian touches such as grappa and gremolata , a garnish of sage, lemon and garlic. Since turkey has a tendency to dry out, the brining step is well worth the extra time and effort.*

Brine

1 cup kosher salt

¼ cup sugar

1 gallon water

1 turkey, approximately 12 pounds, backbone removed, butterflied open (ask the butcher to do this for you) reserving the backbone and neck for gravy

Gravy

1 turkey back

1 turkey neck

2 tablespoons olive oil

1 cup water

1 small onion, cut into chunks

1 carrot, cut into chunks

1 large stalk celery, cut into chunks

1 bay leaf

¼ teaspoon peppercorns, lightly crushed

Turkey

1 head garlic, cut in half crosswise

2 tablespoons olive oil

¼ cup grappa

2 tablespoons fresh sage, coarsely chopped

2 tablespoons fresh rosemary, coarsely chopped

1 teaspoon sea salt

1 tablespoon freshly ground black pepper

Gremolata

2 tablespoons fresh sage, finely chopped

2 tablespoons lemon zest, finely chopped

2 tablespoon garlic, finely chopped

TO MAKE THE BRINE: Put the salt, sugar and water in a large pot. Bring the solution to a boil over high heat. Let cool and refrigerate the mixture overnight.

Remove the brine from the refrigerator. Place the prepared turkey in a large pot and add the brining solution to cover the bird by 1 inch. Add additional cold water if needed to cover. Brine for 8 to 10 hours in the refrigerator.

TO MAKE THE GRAVY: Preheat the oven to 425°F.

In a roasting pan, coat the turkey backbone and neck with 1 tablespoon of the olive oil . Roast, turning once, until well browned, 30 to 45 minutes. Transfer to a medium-sized stockpot, add cold water to cover the turkey parts by 2 inches, and bring to a boil over high heat. Reduce the heat to low and let simmer. Skim off any fat or foam that rises to the surface.

Pour off any excess fat from the roasting pan and place the pan on the stovetop over medium-high heat. Add 1 cup of water and scrape the browned bits off the bottom of the pan. Pour the liquid into the stockpot with the turkey back and neck.

Return the roasting pan to the stove over medium-high heat and add the remaining 1 tablespoon of oil. Add the onion, carrot, and celery and sauté until lightly browned, about 10 minutes. Add the bay leaf and peppercorns and cook until the vegetables are softened, about 15 minutes. Add to the stockpot with the turkey back and neck.

Bring the stockpot contents to a boil over high heat. Reduce the heat to low and let simmer uncovered for about 3 hours. Strain the stock through a fine mesh sieve and discard the solids. Let cool and refrigerate overnight.

When well chilled, use a large spoon to remove any solid-ified fat and discard.

The stock is now ready to be reduced for gravy. Bring the stock to a boil over high heat, reduce the heat to low, and gently simmer. Reduce the stock until thickened to the desired consistency. Season to taste with salt and pepper. Keep warm until ready to serve.

Preheat oven to 350°F.

Remove the turkey from the brining solution and pat well to dry. Have ready a roasting pan large enough to hold the butterflied bird. Place the split garlic bulb in the center of the pan and pour oil over and around the garlic.

Pour the grappa over the turkey and rub it all over. Rub the turkey with the sage, rosemary, salt and pepper. Place the bird in the pan over the garlic, skin side up. Cook for 2½ hours or until an instant-read thermometer registers 180°F when inserted into the thigh.

TO MAKE THE GREMOLATA: Combine the sage, lemon zest, and the garlic. Set aside.

When the turkey is cooked, remove from the oven and transfer the turkey to a serving platter. Sprinkle with Gre-molata and let the bird rest for 15 minutes. Serve with the gravy on the side.

· ·

Praline Pumpkin Pie

SERVES 8 *Pumpkin pie lovers will renew their vows after trying this recipe which has surprise praline-like layer between the crust and the filling.*

a

- 2 tablespoons butter
- ⅓ cup pecans
- 1 cup brown sugar, packed
- 1 unbaked pie shell
- 1 teaspoon cinnamon
- ¾ teaspoon ginger
- ½ teaspoon nutmeg
- ¼ teaspoon cloves
- ¼ teaspoon allspice
- ½ teaspoon salt
- 1½ cups canned pumpkin (not pumpkin pie filling)
- 3 eggs, lightly beaten
- 1 cup milk
- 2 tablespoons corn syrup
- 2 tablespoons melted butter

Preheat oven to 375°F.

In a small nonstick pan, melt the butter and add the pecans and ⅓ cup brown sugar. Stir to combine and continue cooking until the mixture starts to bubble. Continue cooking for a minute or two until the mixture starts to get thick. Immediately pour into the unbaked pie shell, being careful not to let the mixture come into contact with your skin.

In a small bowl, combine the cinnamon, ginger, nutmeg, cloves, allspice and salt and mix together until well combined. In the bowl of a KitchenAid stand mixer, add the pumpkin, eggs, remaining ⅔ cup brown sugar, milk, corn syrup and melted butter. Add the spice mixture and beat on low speed to combine. Increase the mixer to medium speed and beat until the ingredients are well blended for approximately 1 to 2 minutes.

Pour the filling over the praline mixture and bake at 375°F for 50 minutes

Note: Bake on cookie sheet lined with foil in case there are any spills.

Red and Green Apple Pie

SERVES 8 *This unique apple pie from cookbook author Dede Wilson calls for two different kinds of apples. Dried cranberries and walnuts give it a little extra punch. Try mixing tart Granny Smiths with sweet red apples such as Northern Spy, Empire or Cortland.*

Crust

2½ cups all purpose flour

2 teaspoons sugar

1 teaspoon salt

1 cup (2 sticks) chilled unsalted butter, cut into ½-inch pieces

4 tablespoons ice water, plus more as needed

Filling

8 medium-sized apples (use a mixture of half red and half green apples), thinly sliced (should yield 8 cups of slices)

¾ cup sugar

½ cup dried cranberries

½ cup roasted walnuts, finely chopped

1 teaspoon freshly squeezed lemon juice

½ teaspoon cinnamon

1 tablespoon all purpose flour

3 tablespoons unsalted butter, cut into small pieces

Topping

1 tablespoon milk

1 tablespoon sugar

Pinch cinnamon

TO MAKE THE CRUST: In the bowl of a KitchenAid food processor with a multipurpose blade, add the flour, sugar, and salt and process until thoroughly mixed. Add butter and pulse 3 to 4 times, 2 to 3 seconds each time, until crumbly. Sprinkle in 3 tablespoons of the water and pulse 1 to 3 times, 2 to 3 seconds each time, or until mixture pulls away from sides of bowl and the dry ingredients are moistened. Moist clumps should form; add an additional tablespoon of water if mixture is dry. On a floured surface, gather the dough into a ball, divide into two pieces and flatten into discs. Wrap the dough in plastic and refrigerate at least 1 hour. (Can be prepared 2 days ahead. Keep refrigerated. Let dough soften slightly at room temperature before rolling out.)

TO MAKE THE FILLING: Preheat oven to 400°F. Spray a 9-inch deep-dish glass pie plate with Pam or other spray coating. Toss together the apple slices, sugar, cranberries, walnuts, lemon juice, and cinnamon and let sit 15 minutes. Fold in the flour.

Roll out 1 dough disc on a floured work surface to a 12-inch round. Transfer to the pie plate. Spoon the filling into the crust and dot with butter.

Roll out the second dough disc on a floured work surface to a 13-inch round. Cut out about 10 circles towards the center of the crust using a ½-inch round cutter. Drape the dough over the filling. Trim the dough overhang to ½-inch. Press the top crust and bottom crust together at the edge to seal. Fold the edge under and crimp the edges decoratively.

TO MAKE THE TOPPING: Brush the piecrust with milk. Combine the sugar and cinnamon in a small bowl and sprinkle evenly over the pie. Place the pie on a parchment-lined sheet pan. Place in the oven, reduce the temperature to 375°F and bake for about 50 minutes or until the crust is golden brown and the filling is bubbly.

Cool on a rack for 30 minutes to allow the juices to thicken. Serve warm or at room temperature. (Can be made 6 hours ahead. Let stand at room temperature). Serve with vanilla ice cream.

Chocolate Caramel Pecan Pie

MAKES ONE 9-INCH PIE *Adding a caramel component to chocolate pecan pie produces extraordinary results. Use the highest quality chocolate you can find—your guests will beg you for the recipe*

½ cup water

1½ cups sugar

½ cup (4 ounces) butter, cut into small pieces

14 ounces evaporated milk

2 ounces unsweetened chocolate, chopped

2 cups pecans, chopped

1 pre-baked 9-inch pie shell

1 cup whole pecans

Preheat the oven to 475°F.

Boil the water and sugar together until it caramelizes, about 15 minutes. Remove from the heat and pour the mixture into a bowl. Slowly stir in the butter and milk.

Let cool for 5 minutes. Stir in the chocolate and mix until smooth. Let cool for 10 to 15 minutes. Stir in the chopped nuts.

Pour the chocolate-caramel mixture into the pie shell. Arrange the whole pecans in a pretty pattern over the top.

Bake for 10 minutes, until the filling is set, and let cool for 1 hour. Cut into slices and serve with vanilla bean ice cream.

The Great American Pumpkin Ice Cream Pie

MAKES ONE 9-INCH PIE *During fall, it's easy to find pumpkin ice cream at supermarkets, making it a cinch to create this wonderful ice cream pie whose crust is a delicious combination of chocolate sandwich cookies and ginger snaps.*

24 ginger snap cookies
 (approximately 1 _ inches in diameter)

¼ cup melted butter

10 chocolate sandwich cookies

8 cups pumpkin ice cream

1 cup finely chopped pecan brittle (store-bought)

Add the ginger cookies into the bowl of a food processor fitted with the multipurpose blade. Process until you have fine crumbs. Add the melted butter and process until just incorporated. Transfer the mixture into a pie shell and press the crumbs into the bottom and sides with your fingers to make a crust. Process the chocolate sandwich cookies to crumbs in the food processor. Pour the chocolate crumbs on top of the ginger crust to create a second layer.

Using a small ice cream scoop, fill the ginger-chocolate cookie crust with balls of ice cream, mounding the ice cream towards the middle of the pie. Sprinkle the pecan brittle over the top of the ice cream.

Keep the pie frozen before serving.

Cranberry Pecan Pumpkin Upside Down Cakes

SERVES 6 *These pretty little mini pumpkin cakes are topped with a slightly gooey caramel topping, cranberries, and pecans—wonderful dessert for Thanksgiving or any fall dinner party. Large silicone muffin molds work beautifully for this recipe if you have them.*

    6 tablespoons unsalted butter

    ½ cup firmly packed brown sugar

    1 cup cranberries

    ½ cup coarsely chopped pecans, toasted

    1 large egg

    ½ cup pumpkin purée

    3 tablespoons vegetable oil

    ¾ cup all purpose flour

    ½ cup sugar

    ¾ teaspoon baking powder

    ½ teaspoon cinnamon

    ⅛ teaspoon salt

    Chantilly Cream (recipe follows)

Preheat the oven to 350°F. Grease the insides of 6 large muffin pans.

Melt the butter in a small saucepot over medium heat until hot. Add the brown sugar and whisk until smooth. Pour the brown sugar mixture into the bottom of each of the pans.

In a medium bowl combine the cranberries and pecans. Spoon the mixture into the muffin pans on top of the brown sugar mixture.

In the bowl of a KitchenAid stand mixer, fitted with the whip attachment, whisk together the egg, pumpkin purée, and the oil.

In a separate bowl, sift together the flour, sugar, baking powder, cinnamon, and salt. Stir the flour mixture into the pumpkin mixture and using the paddle attachment, mix until just blended. Spoon the batter evenly over the cranberry pecan toppings.

Bake for 15 minutes until a skewer inserted in the middle comes out clean. Let cool for 15 minutes. Place a baking sheet on top of the muffin pan. Invert the pan and baking sheet together. Carefully remove the muffin pan, transfer the cakes to individual plates and serve with Chantilly Cream (recipe follows).

Chantilly Cream

MAKES 2 CUPS

    1 cup heavy (whipping) cream

    3 tablespoons sugar

    ½ teaspoon vanilla extract

In the bowl of a KitchenAid mixer fitted with the whisk attachment, combine all of the ingredients and beat at high speed until soft peaks form. Refrigerate until you are ready to use.

Leftovers

Devonshire Sandwich

SERVES 6 *The host of* The Holiday Table *television series, Chris Fennimore, brought us the perfect antidote to dried-out, leftover turkey sandwiches with this authentic Pittsburgh favorite.*

Cream Sauce

¾ stick (6 tablespoons) butter, melted

1 cup flour

2 cups chicken broth

2 cups hot milk

¼ pound Cheddar cheese, grated

1 teaspoon salt

Sandwich

6 slices toast, crusts trimmed off

18 slices crisp bacon

30 thin slices cooked turkey breast

Melted butter

Parmesan cheese

Paprika

Preheat oven to 450°F.

TO MAKE THE CREAM SAUCE: Melt the butter in a deep saucepan and add the flour, stirring constantly. Add the chicken broth and the hot milk, stirring constantly. Add the cheese and the salt. Bring to a boil, cooking slowly for 20 minutes and stirring constantly. Cool to lukewarm. Beat with a whisk until smooth before using. This makes enough sauce for 6 Devonshire sandwiches.

TO MAKE THE SANDWICHES: Into an individual oven-proof casserole dish, place 1 slice of toast, then top with 3 slices of bacon. Add 5 thin slices of cooked turkey breast. Cover completely with cream sauce. Sprinkle with a little melted butter. Stir together the parmesan cheese and paprika in a small bowl and sprinkle over the butter. Repeat for the other 5 sandwiches. Bake for 10 to 15 minutes or until golden brown.

Turkey Croquettes

SERVES 4 *Here is a unique and delicious use of Thanksgiving leftovers. While croquettes are often deep fried in oil, this recipe calls for baking them in the oven for healthier results.*

2 cups cooked turkey meat

1 cup stuffing

1 cup turkey gravy

1 egg

1 lemon, juiced

½ cup breadcrumbs

Cranberry sauce as an accompaniment.

Preheat the oven to 350°F.

Put the turkey, gravy and stuffing in the bowl of a KitchenAid food processor fitted with the multipurpose blade and pulse until the mixture is still coarse but well blended.

Measure out ⅓ cup of the mixture and roll it into a ball. Beat together the egg and the juice of 1 lemon. Dip the ball first in the egg and then roll in the breadcrumbs. Roll each croquette gently between your palms into the traditional cone shape and place on a greased baking pan. Repeat for all the croquettes.

Bake at 350°F for 30 minutes or until golden brown. Heat the cranberry sauce in a pan and serve on the side as a sauce.

Savory Bread Pudding

SERVES 6 TO 8 *You'll love this simple way to put new life into leftover stuffing. It takes the great flavors of your stuffing, adds a healthy dose of parmesan cheese, and voila! No one will believe they're eating leftovers.*

> 6 cups stuffing
>
> 2 cups milk
>
> 1 cup cream
>
> 6 large eggs
>
> ¼ teaspoon salt
>
> Ground pepper
>
> 2 heaping tablespoons fresh sage
> and oregano, chopped
>
> ¾ cup grated parmesan cheese

Preheat the oven to 350°F.

In a lightly greased 9-inch baking pan or casserole dish, place the stuffing evenly in the bottom. In a large mixing bowl, whisk together the milk, cream, eggs, salt, pepper, chopped herbs, and parmesan cheese. Pour the mixture over the stuffing.

Bake until a small knife inserted in the center almost comes out clean, about 45 minutes.

Turkey Chili

SERVE 6 TO 8 *It is no wonder that turkey chili has gotten so popular—it cooks quickly and is bursting with intense flavors. Serve with a variety of toppings on the side, such as shredded cheddar cheese, finely chopped onions, or crackers and your guests can choose what they like.*

> 1 tablespoon olive oil
>
> 1 medium onion, chopped
>
> 2 cloves garlic, minced
>
> Three 14½-ounce cans black beans
>
> Two 14-ounce cans diced tomatoes
>
> 1 cup tomato sauce
>
> 1 pound cooked turkey breast,
> cut up into ½-inch cubes
>
> 1½ teaspoons cumin
>
> ¼ teaspoon red pepper flakes, plus more if needed
>
> ⅓ cup parsley, chopped
>
> ⅓ cup cilantro, chopped
>
> Salt
>
> Pepper

Heat a 4- to 5-quart soup pot or Dutch oven over medium heat and add the olive oil. Add the onion and the garlic and sauté until soft.

Add the black beans, tomatoes, tomato sauce, turkey, cumin, and red pepper flakes and cook over medium heat until hot. Sir in the chopped parsley and cilantro. Season to taste with salt and pepper.

Chanukah

Zucchini or Cauliflower Latkes

MAKES 12 TO 14 TWO-INCH PANCAKES

When we asked Mitchell Davis, author of The Mensch Chef *and* Kitchen Sense, *to come up with some alternative latke recipes, he brought us two delicious variations, one made with cauliflower and one with zucchini.*

1 large Yukon gold potato (about 8 ounces), scrubbed clean

1 pound zucchini or 1 pound cauliflower, steamed till tender

1 medium yellow onion, peeled

2 large eggs

1 large egg white

3 tablespoons bread crumbs

2 teaspoons potato starch or cornstarch

¼ cup chopped fresh flat-leaf parsley (or 2 tablespoons chopped fresh dill)

2 teaspoons kosher salt

½ teaspoon freshly ground black pepper

½ to ¾ cup vegetable oil, for frying

Optional toppings

Sour cream

Applesauce

In a preheated 400°F oven, roast the potato for 30 minutes until partially cooked. Set aside and let cool.

TO MAKE ZUCCHINI LATKE BATTER: Cut off the ends of the zucchini and, using a medium size shredding disc (4mm), shred in a KitchenAid food processor. Wrap the shredded zucchini in a clean kitchen towel and twist to wring out excess liquid.

Using the same shredding disc, shred the potato and onion. In a large mixing bowl, mix together the zucchini, potato, onion, eggs, egg white, bread crumbs, potato starch, parsley, salt, and pepper and combine well. The batter is now ready to fry.

TO MAKE CAULIFLOWER LATKE BATTER: Using a medium size shredding disc (4mm), shred the cauliflower, potato, and onion in a KitchenAid food processor. In a large mixing bowl, mix together the cauliflower, potato, onion, eggs, egg white, bread crumbs, potato starch, parsley, salt, and pepper and combine well. The batter is now ready to fry.

TO FRY THE LATKES: In a large frying pan, heat ⅛ inch of oil over medium-high heat. Line a clean plate or baking sheet with paper towels.

Using about ¼ cup of the zucchini or cauliflower mixture, form a small patty and place in the frying pan. Use a spatula to gently press down on the pancake to compact and flatten it. Repeat to fill the pan with pancakes, leaving enough room between them so they will cook without touching. Cook until the underside is nicely browned, about 5 minutes. Do not cook too quickly or the insides will be raw. Lower the heat if the edges begin to burn.

Flip each pancake with a spatula, being careful not to break them. Press them down gently again with a spatula and fry for another 4 minutes or so until brown. Transfer to the paper towel-lined plate.

Serve immediately. Latkes are traditionally served with sour cream and applesauce.

Traditional Potato Pancakes (Latkes)

MAKES EIGHT 3-INCH LATKES

This is the dish most closely associated with Chanukah and probably the most loved. At many celebrations, you will find people standing over the frying pan, never giving the latkes a chance to make it to a serving platter. The big secret to making a great latke is squeezing out the moisture from the potatoes and onions.

- ¾ pound russet potatoes, peeled
- ½ medium onion
- ¼ cup flour
- ¾ to 1 teaspoon salt
- 1 egg
- Vegetable oil for frying

Using the shredding disc of the food processor, shred the potatoes and onions. Transfer to a strainer and wring out all the excess moisture from the potatoes and onion. Place the potatoes and onion into a mixing bowl and stir in the flour, salt, and egg.

Heat a large sauté pan. Add vegetable oil to the pan approximately ¼-inch-deep.

Over medium-low heat, drop spoonfuls of the mixture into the pan according to the size of latke you want (average size is 3 inches diameter). Flatten with the back of a spoon. Fry until crisp and cooked through, approximately 12 to 15 minutes. While frying, adjust the heat in order to give the potatoes enough time to cook thoroughly and to brown properly. Drain on paper towels. Serve warm with apple sauce and sour cream.

Cheese Latkes

By Mitchell Davis. Adapted from *The Mensch Chef* (Clarkson Potter, 2002).

MAKES SIXTEEN 3-INCH LATKES

These sweet pancakes, with their creamy cheeses laced with vanilla, make an irresistible breakfast treat or dessert. Farmer cheese, also called dry curd cottage cheese, is cottage cheese with the moisture removed.

- 1 cup farmer cheese
- ¼ cup cream cheese, at room temperature
- 3 eggs
- 1 cup milk
- 1 cup matzo meal
- 1 teaspoon kosher salt
- ¼ cup sugar
- 1 teaspoon pure vanilla extract
- 5 tablespoons unsalted butter

In the bowl of the KitchenAid stand mixer, beat together the farmer cheese and cream cheese until smooth. Add in the eggs, milk, matzo meal, salt, sugar, and vanilla and continue beating until a smooth mixture is formed. Let sit for about 20 minutes until the batter firms up.

Heat 1 tablespoon of the butter in a large frying pan set over medium-high heat. Pour ¼ cup of the batter into the pan, and repeat, leaving enough room between each pancake to cook without touching. Cook until the pancakes have browned on the bottom and begin to bubble slightly, about 4 minutes. Carefully flip over and cook for an additional 2 to 3 minutes, until browned.

Transfer to a clean plate or cookie sheet and keep warm. Continue frying the latkes, adding more butter as necessary and being careful not to let the pan get so hot that the latkes burn before they are cooked through. (Take the pan off the heat for a minute or two between batches.) Serve warm.

Beer Braised Beef Brisket with Cranberries and Mushrooms

SERVES 8 TO 10 *When cooked correctly, this is one of the most tender and flavorful cuts of beef imaginable. It is often found at the Chanukah table because it goes so well with potato pancakes (latkes). Brisket is best when treated to long, slow cooking. Ideally, make it the day ahead so you have time to carve the meat when it is still cold and remove excess fat.*

> One 5 to 6 pound brisket (see Note)
>
> Salt
>
> Pepper
>
> 2 large onions, thinly sliced
>
> 12 ounces dark beer
>
> 1 tablespoon brown sugar
>
> 2 tablespoons tomato paste
>
> ¾ cup dried cranberries
>
> 1 pound mushrooms (button, cremini or Portobello) sliced thickly

Preheat the oven to 325°F.

Season the brisket generously with salt and pepper. Lay half the onions on the bottom of a large roasting pan or heavy braiser. Place the brisket (fat side up) on the onions and top the brisket with the remaining onions.

In a small bowl, mix together the beer, brown sugar, and tomato paste and pour it over the brisket. Cover the roasting pan with a lid or aluminum foil and bake for about 3 hours. Add the cranberries and mushrooms, cover, and continue cooking until the meat is very tender and has no resistance when pierced with a fork, about 30 minutes more.

Wrap the brisket in aluminum foil. Reserve the pan juices in a bowl and cover with aluminum foil. When cool, place both in the refrigerator, preferably overnight.

Just before serving, preheat the oven to 350°F.

With a sharp knife, remove any excess fat from the cold brisket and slice thinly *against the grain*. Arrange the slices in a roasting pan or large, shallow casserole. Discard any fat from the reserved juices. Pour the juices over the beef.

Place into the oven and reheat until warmed through, about 30 minutes. (This can also be done on the stove top over a low flame.) If necessary add more water or broth to create more juices. Serve warm.

Note: There is debate over how much fat to leave on the brisket prior to cooking. We suggest leaving at least a thin layer of fat because it adds lots of flavor.

Slow-Cooked Short Ribs with Wild Mushrooms and Dried Fruit

By Mitchell Davis, author of *Kitchen Sense* and *The Mensch Chef*, published by Clarkson Potter.

SERVES 6 *With Chanukah occurring in late winter, this is a great choice for a nighttime celebration. Made in a slow cooker, the results are fall-off-the-bone beef short ribs, enhanced with dried fruit, wild mushrooms, and both sweet and white potatoes.*

5 pounds beef short ribs or flanken

1 tablespoon kosher salt

1 teaspoon freshly ground black pepper

¾ cup flour

3 tablespoons peanut oil,
   chicken schmaltz, or beef schmaltz

1 large yellow onion, sliced

1 large garlic clove, minced

¼ cup dry red wine

2 tablespoons tomato paste

1 bay leaf

½ cup dried apricots

½ cup dried prunes

¼ pound wild mushrooms

¾ pound white potatoes,
   peeled and cut in large chunks

¾ pound sweet potatoes,
   peeled and cut in large chunks

½ pound carrots, cut in 1-inch slices

Season the short ribs with the salt and pepper. Coat with flour and shake off any excess. In a large frying pan set over high heat, pour in the peanut oil and heat until the pan is very hot. Sear the ribs for 4 to 5 minutes per side until well-browned on all sides. Transfer to a KitchenAid slow cooker.

Add the onion, garlic, red wine, tomato paste, bay leaf, apricots, prunes, mushrooms, white potatoes, sweet potatoes, and carrots and cook for 8 to 9 hours according to the slow cooker instructions, until the vegetables are tender and the meat is falling off the bone.

Easy Apple Almond Cheese Tart

SERVES 8 *In keeping with the tradition of eating cheese at Chanukah, this is a wonderful dessert with an easy crust, a sweet cream cheese filling, and a luscious apple almond topping.*

Crust

½ cup butter, softened,

⅓ cup sugar

¼ teaspoon vanilla

1 cup flour

Cheese Filling

1 package (8 ounce) cream cheese, softened

¼ cup sugar

1 egg

¼ teaspoon vanilla

Apple Topping

4 cups peeled and cored apples,
   sliced ¼-inch-thick

⅓ cup sugar

¼ teaspoon cinnamon

⅓ cup sliced almonds

Preheat oven to 350°F.

TO MAKE THE CRUST: In the bowl of a KitchenAid stand mixer fitted with the paddle attachment, cream together the butter and sugar for 2 to 3 minutes. Scrape down the bowl, and beat in the vanilla. Turn the speed to low, add the flour and mix just until blended. Using your fingers, press the dough onto the bottom and sides of a 9-inch spring form pan or a tart pan with a removable bottom. Bake for 10 minutes until light brown.

TO MAKE THE CHEESE FILLING: Raise the oven temperature to 425°F. After cleaning the stand mixer bowl and paddle, beat together cream cheese, sugar, egg and vanilla. Pour the mixture into the prepared crust.

TO MAKE THE APPLE TOPPING: In a bowl, mix together the apples, sugar and cinnamon. Layer on top of the batter. Place on a foil-lined cookie sheet and bake for 25 minutes. Sprinkle the almonds over the apples and bake for 10 minutes.

Transfer the cookie sheet to a wire rack and let cool for 20 minutes. Release the springform side and transfer the tart to a serving platter.

Rugelach

By Mitchell Davis. Adapted from *Kitchen Sense* (Clarkson Potter, 2006) and *The Mensch Chef* (Clarkson Potter, 2002).

MAKES 4 DOZEN *Rugelach, a crescent-shaped cookie that melts in your mouth, is a beloved Jewish specialty known for its delicious cream cheese cookie dough and wide variety of fillings. In this recipe, Mitchell Davis, Vice President of the James Beard Foundation, gives us two choices of fillings.*

Chocolate Filling

¾ cup sugar

½ cup chopped walnuts

⅓ cup unflavored toasted bread crumbs

½ cup cocoa powder

4 tablespoons unsalted butter, melted and cooled

¼ cup milk or soy milk

1 teaspoon pure vanilla extract

½ cup semi-sweet chocolate chips

Lemon and Almond filling

1 cup whole almonds (6 ounces), with skins on

½ cup sugar

Zest of 1 lemon (about 2 teaspoons)

½ cup apricot, raspberry, or currant jam,
    or your preference

Cream Cheese dough

6 ounces cream cheese, at room temperature

8 ounces (1 cup) unsalted butter,
    at room temperature

1½ cups unbleached all-purpose flour,
    plus more as needed

About 2 cups Chocolate or
    Lemon and Almond filling (recipes above)

1 egg beaten with 1 teaspoon cold water (egg wash)

2 tablespoons crystallized sugar or Sugar in the Raw

TO MAKE THE CHOCOLATE FILLING: In the bowl of a KitchenAid food processor fitted with a multipurpose blade, pulse the sugar, nuts, and bread crumbs just until the walnuts are ground fine. Be careful not to over process. Transfer to a mixing bowl, add the cocoa powder, melted butter, milk, and vanilla, and stir to combine. Stir in the chocolate chips and set aside.

TO MAKE THE LEMON AND ALMOND FILLING: Preheat the oven to 350°F. Spread out the almonds on a cookie sheet and toast for 10 to 15 minutes or until you can smell a strong, toasted nut smell, and the color of the nuts has darkened. Toss the nuts with a heat-resistant spatula once or twice to be sure they toast evenly. Let cool.

In the bowl of a KitchenAid food processor fitted with a multipurpose blade, pulse the sugar, toasted almonds, and lemon zest just until the nuts are finely chopped and uniform. Be careful not to over process. Set aside.

TO MAKE THE CREAM CHEESE DOUGH: In the bowl of a KitchenAid stand mixer, beat the cream cheese and butter until well combined. Add the flour and continue to mix to form a soft dough, adding more flour as needed. Chill the dough for at least 2 hours before rolling out and shaping. (The dough can also be frozen for up to 2 months and defrosted in the refrigerator before using.)

Preheat the oven to 425°F.

TO SHAPE THE RUGELACH: Divide the dough into 4 even balls. Refrigerate all but the ball of dough you are working with. Roll the dough into a 10-inch circle, using a generous amount of flour to keep the dough from sticking. Using a pastry brush, remove any excess flour clinging to the rolled out dough.

If making Lemon and Almond Rugelach, spread the rolled out dough with ¼ of the jam (about 2 tablespoons). Sprinkle with ¼ of the lemon almond mixture (about ½ cup).

If making Chocolate Rugelach, spread ¼ of the Chocolate Filling over the rolled out dough (about ½ cup).

Cut the dough circle into quarters. Divide each of these quarters into three equal isosceles triangles. Roll up each triangle, starting from the base and working toward the point. Bend to shape into crescents and transfer to a parchment- or silicone mat- lined cookie sheet, making sure the point of the dough triangle stays tucked underneath.

Repeat with the remaining dough and filling. You will probably need two cookie sheets to accommodate all of the cookies. Leave about 1 inch between the cookies because they will rise and straighten out while they bake.

Brush the cookies with the egg wash and sprinkle with the crystallized sugar. Bake for 15 to 20 minutes, until the dough has puffed and the cookies have browned. Some of the filling may seep out while baking.

Using a spatula, transfer the rugelach to a wire rack while they are still warm so the melted jam and/or sugar won't harden to the cookie sheet. Let cool completely and store in an airtight container for up to 5 days.

Christmas

Appetizers

Asiago and Parmesan Cheese Crisps

MAKES ABOUT 30 CRISPS *These crunchy little cheese crisps are the ultimate in simplicity. They are an elegant garnish for salads or they an be served as a light appetizer. Try different herbs and spices or experiment with different shapes—there are endless variations.*

> 4 ounces Asiago cheese
> 4 ounces parmesan cheese
> Black pepper

Preheat the oven to 350°F.

Using the medium shredding disc of the KitchenAid food processor, shred the Asiago and parmesan cheese. Mix the cheese together in a bowl with a pinch of black pepper. See Flavor Variations for herbs and spices which can be added at this point.

Line a baking sheet with parchment paper and lightly grease (alternatively, use a Silpat sheet, which works best). Spoon the cheese mixture in 1-tablespoon-sized mounds onto the prepared baking sheet, making sure to place them 4 inches apart. Using your fingers, pat the mounds into 3½-inch circles or ovals in an even thickness.

Bake for 4 to 5 minutes or until the cheese is melted and any bubbles that form turn into a crunchy light golden crust. They should be golden in color and lacy in appearance. See Shape Variations for different options.

Let the cheese crisps cool completely on the baking sheet. Transfer the crisps carefully using a thin spatula to a paper towel-lined plate.

FLAVOR VARIATIONS

ROSEMARY CHEESE CRISPS: Add 2 tablespoons of finely chopped fresh rosemary leaves to the cheese mix.

CUMIN CHEESE CRISPS: Add 1 teaspoon cumin, caraway, or fennel seeds to the cheese mix.

NUT CHEESE CRISPS: Sprinkle the top of each cheese circle with some chopped nuts of your choice before baking.

SHAPE VARIATIONS

CHEESE BASKETS: Remove the baked cheese circles from the oven and allow to cool for 1 minute. Remove them from the baking sheet using a thin spatula and place them over a shot glass, egg carton, wine cork, miniature muffin tin, or anything to form a tulip shape. Let cool and remove from the form.

LARGE BASKETS: Follow the same procedure as above using a large cheese circle. Drape over a coffee cup, custard cup, or drinking glass. Let cool and remove from the form.

CHEESE ROLLS: Drape warm cheese crisps over a dowel or rolling pin.

CHEESE CONES: Press warm cheese crisp over an ice cream cone

Caramelized Onion Dip

MAKES 1¼ CUPS *Once you taste the deep natural sweetness of caramelized onions in this classic treat, you'll never dip your chip into anything else. Great with both vegetables and traditional potato chips.*

- 2 cups chopped onions
- 3 tablespoons light olive oil
- 1 cup sour cream
- Salt
- Pepper

In a heavy-bottomed sauté pan, cook the onions in the olive oil over medium heat for about 20 minutes, stirring ever 4 minutes or so, until the onions are a rich golden brown.

Let cool to room temperature. Fold the onions into the sour cream and season liberally with salt and pepper. Store in a covered container and refrigerate overnight or up to 3 days. The flavor improves significantly if the dip sits overnight.

Creamy Sun Dried Tomato Dip

MAKES 1⅛ CUPS *Instead of paying a premium for pre-mixed dips, try making them yourself. They are simple to prepare, use natural, fresh ingredients, and, like this one, they taste better than anything you could buy at the store.*

- ¼ cup sun dried tomatoes
- ¼ cup basil
- 8 ounces goat cheese at room temperature
- ¼ cup half and half, or as needed

In the work bowl of a KitchenAid food processor, chop the sun dried tomatoes and basil. Add the goat cheese, and pulse until combined. While the motor is running, slowly pour in the half and half until the mixture reaches the desired consistency. Refrigerate overnight.

Serve with crudités and crackers or spread on crostini.

Easy Homemade Gravlax

SERVES 20 *Gravlax has its roots in Scandinavia and means "buried salmon." It's typically cured for three days in a salt, sugar, and dill mixture. People who make it for the first time find it surprisingly easy to make.*

- 1 side of salmon, approximately 4 pounds, skin on and pin bones removed
- 8 juniper berries, crushed (optional)
- 2 teaspoon black peppercorns, crushed
- ¼ cup Kosher salt
- ¼ cup sugar
- 1 cup plus 2 tablespoons fresh dill, chopped
- ¼ cup gin
- 10 slices dark pumpernickel bread
- ¼ cup (½ stick) unsalted butter

Line a large glass baking dish with enough plastic wrap to cover the bottom completely and hang over the sides. Place the salmon, skin side down, into the dish.

Mix together the crushed juniper berries and peppercorns, the salt, and the sugar and sprinkle the mixture evenly over the salmon. Spread 1 cup of the chopped dill over the fish. Drizzle the gin over the fish as evenly as possible.

Wrap the plastic up and over the fish. Place a pan or plate that fits inside the baking dish over the fish. Weigh down the fish by placing heavy canned goods on top of the pan or plate.

Refrigerate for three days. When it is ready to serve, the fish should have lost its translucence. Unwrap the fish and scrape off the dill, salt, and sugar. Slice the salmon very thinly on the bias and remove the skin.

Arrange the gravlax on a serving platter along with a crock of sweet butter and slices of pumpernickel bread. Garnish with the 2 tablespoons fresh dill and serve.

Brie and Goat Cheese Soufflé

SERVES 6 *This is another recipe Jean Pierre Brehier shared with us: an easy first course that is both elegant and delicious. The brie, goat cheese, and sun dried tomatoes along with the tangy sourdough bread and garlic make every bite memorable.*

- 2½ cups half-and-half
- ¼ cup sun dried tomatoes, cut into small dice
- 2 tablespoons chopped garlic
- 6 large egg yolks
- 4 ounces Brie (rind removed), diced into cubes
- 4 ounces crumbled goat cheese
- 2 cups sourdough bread, crust removed and cut into ½-inch cubes

Preheat oven to 375°F.

In a saucepan, heat the half-and-half, sun dried tomatoes and the garlic. In a glass bowl, mix together the eggs, salt and pepper. Stir the warm half-and-half mixture into the eggs.

Butter the inside of six ramekins (5 to 8 ounces each) or use a non-stick spray. In a glass bowl, mix together the bread and the cheese and divide equally into the buttered molds. Pour the half-and-half mixture over the top of each ramekin and let stand for a couple minutes. Using a spoon, make sure that all the bread is covered with the half-and-half mixture.

Transfer the ramekins to the oven and bake for 15 to 20 minutes or until they are golden brown. Let rest at room temperature for at least 20 minutes. Run a knife around the edges to unmold and serve warm.

Mushroom and Goat Cheese Bites

MAKES 15 PIECES *This recipe takes advantage of a great convenience product— mini Fillo shells—which are an attractive presentation at any gathering. It's also a great do-ahead dish since they can be made a day ahead and put into the oven just before your guests arrive.*

2 shallots

1 garlic clove

1½ cups mushrooms, such as cremini or button

2 teaspoons olive oil

2 tablespoons chicken stock

Salt

Pepper

1 tablespoons fresh basil, chopped (or 1 teaspoon dried)

3 tablespoons goat cheese

15 mini Fillo shells

Preheat oven to 350°F.

In the mini bowl of a KitchenAid food processor, process the shallots and garlic until chopped. Transfer the mixture to a bowl. Add the mushrooms to the mini bowl and process until chopped.

In a heated sauté pan, add the olive oil and the shallot–garlic mixture and sauté for 1 minute. Add the chopped mushrooms and continue to sauté for 3 to 5 minutes. Add the chicken stock and simmer until the liquid evaporates. Season to taste with salt and pepper and stir in the basil.

Place 1 rounded teaspoon of filling into each fillo shell. Top with about ½ teaspoon of goat cheese (or to taste). Bake in the oven for 5 minutes. Serve warm.

Pigs in a Blanket

MAKES ABOUT 24 PIECES *Here's an appetizer that never goes out of style and is a sure-fire hit for young and old. Your choice of sausage and mustard will definitely affect the final results, so be sure to check out the many options available and choose your favorite.*

4 tablespoons all-purpose flour

¾ pound puff pastry, defrosted if frozen

1 pound small sausage links (no more than ½-inch-thick), cut into 1½- to 2-inch lengths

2 tablespoons Dijon mustard

1 egg, beaten with 1 tablespoon cold water to make an egg wash

Salt

Pepper

Preheat oven to 425°F.

Lightly dust a work surface with flour and roll out the puff pastry to about ⅛-inch thick. Cut the dough into small triangles 2-inches wide along one side.

Brush the sausage pieces with the mustard. Place a sausage along one edge of the puff pastry and roll it around the sausage. Brush with some of the egg wash and sprinkle with salt and pepper. Repeat with all the sausages and puff pastry triangles.

Transfer to a parchment-lined baking sheet and bake for about 20 minutes. Serve warm.

Roasted Vegetable Terrine with Goat Cheese, Eggplant, and Red Peppers

MAKES 1 SMALL TERRINE *This is a colorful and elegant first course with its beautiful layers of roasted vegetables sandwiched between a goat cheese, honey, and balsamic vinegar spread. Like most terrines, it needs to be made the day before so it has time to sit and compress.*

- 4 Japanese eggplant
- 2 zucchini, approximately 8 inches long
- Olive oil
- Salt
- Pepper
- ¼ cup fresh thyme leaves
- 4 tablespoons balsamic vinegar
- 2 tablespoons light soy sauce
- 1 tablespoon honey
- 3 tablespoons whipping cream
- ½ cup goat cheese
- ½ pound oyster mushrooms
- 2 large red peppers, roasted (see Note)

Preheat oven to 450°F.

Line a 4-by-8-inch loaf pan with enough plastic wrap to hang over the sides of the pan.

PRE-ROAST THE VEGETABLES: Slice the eggplant and zucchini lengthwise into about ⅛-inch-thick long slices and place on a baking sheet. Do not overlap. Brush the vegetables lightly with olive oil. Sprinkle with salt, pepper, and thyme leaves. Place in the oven on the top third rack and bake 15 minutes. Transfer the vegetables to a paper towel-lined plate to drain and cool completely.

Mix the balsamic vinegar, soy sauce, and honey in a small bowl and set aside. Blend together the whipping cream and goat cheese until smooth and set aside.

ASSEMBLE THE TERRINE: Brush the long slices of eggplant with the balsamic mixture and line the bottom of the bread loaf pan with them crosswise, allowing the slices to go up the sides of the pan (they will be folded back to cover the vegetables). Sprinkle with a little pepper. Place a layer of zucchini running lengthwise with the pan on top of the eggplant. Brush with the balsamic mixture. Place half the mushrooms over the zucchini and brush with the balsamic. Spoon the goat cheese over the mushrooms and make a smooth layer. Cover with the remaining mushrooms and brush with the balsamic. Repeat with the red peppers. If the pan is not full, continue alternating layers of vegetables until almost flush with the top of the pan.

Fold the eggplant over the vegetables to seal them in. Fold the plastic wrap over the vegetables to seal.

Place another bread loaf pan on top of the plastic wrap and place a couple of cans of food in the pan to act as a weight. Refrigerate the terrine for at least 12 hours.

Unmold the terrine and place on a serving platter. Serve with crackers and bread.

Note: High quality roasted red peppers are readily available in jars at grocery stores.

Traditional
Holiday Feast

Popovers

MAKES 6 POPOVERS *With their light and airy texture, popovers are a wonderful accompaniment to roast beef and the perfect vehicle to soak up delicious gravies. They need to be served as soon as they come out of they oven, otherwise they tend to fall.*

>   3 eggs
>   1¼ cup milk at room temperature
>   1¼ cup all-purpose flour
>   ¼ teaspoon salt

Preheat the oven to 450°F. Grease popover tins lightly with vegetable oil spray and place in the oven for a few minutes to warm.

In the bowl of a KitchenAid stand mixer, beat the eggs for approximately 3 minutes until lemon colored and foamy. Reduce to the speed to low, add the milk, and mix until just blended. Do not overbeat. Add the flour and the salt all at once. Beat until foamy and smooth on top. Pour the batter into a pitcher and fill the preheated popover pans half-way full with batter.

Bake for 15 minutes, reduce the heat to 350°F and continue to bake for 30 minutes. Remove the popovers with a sharp knife and serve hot.

Holiday Salad with Cranberries and Pecans

SERVES 10 *This colorful salad, dressed with a mildly sweet honey-mustard dressing, is brimming with goodies. For a great do-ahead tip, you can put the salad ingredients together (except the diced avocado) hours ahead of your meal and hold in the refrigerator. Toss with the dressing right before serving.*

>   3 tablespoons rice wine vinegar
>   1 tablespoon mustard
>   1 tablespoon honey
>   1 teaspoon salt
>   ½ cup extra virgin olive oil
>   12 cups mixed salad greens
>   1 avocado, diced into 1-inch cubes
>   ¼ cup dried cranberries
>   ¼ cup toasted pecans, broken into pieces
>   4 ounces goat cheese, cut into small chunks

In a small bowl, whisk together the rice wine vinegar, mustard, honey, and salt. Continue whisking and slowly pour in the olive oil until the mixture is smooth. Adjust seasonings to taste. Set aside.

In a large bowl, combine the greens, avocado, cranberries, pecans and goat cheese. Pour in the dressing and toss slowly until the ingredients are just lightly coated. Serve immediately.

Oyster and Corn Chowder

SERVES 8 TO 10 *Eating oyster stew or chowder on Christmas is a popular tradition in many families. This recipe combines bacon, corn, potatoes, and succulent oysters in a rich cream-based soup. With red and green garnishes of chopped parsley and paprika, it's a festive way to kick off any Christmas feast.*

10 slices bacon, chopped into small pieces

4 tablespoons butter

2 onions, chopped (about 2 cups)

2 stalks celery, chopped

2 medium carrots, peeled and
   sliced into ¼-inch slices

1 cup sweet corn

1½ teaspoons salt

¾ teaspoon white pepper

½ cup flour

6 cups chicken stock

¼ cup chopped parsley

2 cups white potatoes, peeled and
   cut into ½-inch cubes

2 cups half-and-half

1 teaspoon Worcestershire sauce

¼ teaspoon hot sauce

2 pounds shucked oysters with liquid

Chopped parsley and paprika for garnish

In a large soup pot over medium heat, render the bacon until crisp. Transfer the bacon to a paper towel–lined plate and discard the fat. Add the butter to the heated soup pot. Add the onions, celery, carrots, corn, salt and pepper. Sauté for 8 to 10 minutes until the vegetables are tender, stirring occasionally. Stir the flour into the vegetables and continue cooking 5 minutes more on low heat. Add the chicken stock and parsley, raise the heat, and bring to a boil. Lower the heat, add the potatoes, and simmer uncovered for 15 minutes, or until the potatoes are tender. Stir in the half-and-half, Worcestershire sauce and hot sauce. Bring to a low boil and simmer for 5 minutes. *(The chowder can be refrigerated and kept overnight to this point.)* With the soup simmering, add the reserved bacon and the oysters and simmer for approximately 5 minutes or until the edges of the oysters curl. Ladle into soup bowls. Garnish with chopped parsley and pinches of paprika. Serve immediately.

Crown Roast with Prune and Apricot Stuffing

SERVES 10 TO 12 *A crown roast makes a stunning centerpiece for any holiday meal, especially when you are feeding a large crowd. For a festive touch, serve the roast with the frilly paper hats wrapped around each bone and decorate the serving plate with pretty greens and colorful fruit.*

1 loaf challah or other egg bread,
    cut into cubes and dried out

1 cup apricots

1 cup prunes

1 cup brandy

1 cup craisins

1 pork crown roast, 9 to 10 pounds (see Note)

2 sticks butter

2 onions, chopped

1 cup toasted pecan halves

1 teaspoon nutmeg

1 teaspoon cinnamon

½ teaspoon ground cloves

Salt

Pepper

5 garlic cloves, sliced

THE NIGHT BEFORE MAKING THE CROWN ROAST: Cut the challah into one-inch cubes and allow to sit out to dry. Soak the apricots, prunes and craisins in a bowl with the brandy and enough water to cover.

ON THE DAY OF MAKING THE CROWN ROAST: Preheat the oven to 350°F. Let the roast come to room temperature.

To prepare the stuffing, melt the butter in a large skillet. Add the onions and cook until they are soft. Toss the onions with the dried challah, soaked apricots, prunes, and craisins, the toasted pecan halves, nutmeg, cinnamon, cloves, and salt to taste until they are well mixed.

Rub the bones of the roast with the cut side of a garlic clove. Season the roast with salt and pepper. Using a sharp knife, make small cuts in the fat on the outside of the roast and insert slivers of garlic. Transfer the roast to a large roasting tray or pan with a double layer of aluminum foil in the bottom. This will assist in moving the roast to a platter when it is done. Fill the center with stuffing and cover with a disk made from aluminum foil. Also cover the tips of the bones with aluminum foil to avoid burning.

Roast for 45 minutes. Reduce the temperature to 325°F. and continue cooking for another 2 to 2½ hours or until a thermometer registers 165°F. Carefully transfer the roast to a serving platter using the foil on the bottom to keep the stuffing intact.

Note: A crown roast is made from a pork rib roast or rack of pork that is tied into a circle with the ribs standing up. Be sure to order in advance from your butcher who can tie and French it for you. ("Frenched" means to remove the meat from the end of the ribs to expose a clean bone.) Estimate 1 to 2 racks per person.

Herb-Crusted Standing Rib Roast

SERVES 10 *Standing rib roasts are affectionately called the "king of roasts" and have a habit of stealing everyone's attention at holiday gatherings. While this recipe calls for a roast with seven ribs, you can use a smaller piece of meat and adjust the herbs and cooking times appropriately.*

4 cloves garlic

2 sprigs rosemary

5 sprigs thyme

6 sprigs parsley

3 sprigs basil

3 sprigs sage

¼ cup olive oil

Standing rib roast with seven rib bones, trimmed of all but ¼-inch of exterior fat

Kosher salt

Freshly ground pepper

Preheat oven to 450°F.

In a bowl of a KitchenAid food processor fitted with a multipurpose blade, process the garlic, rosemary, thyme, parsley, basil, and sage. With the motor running, slowly add the olive oil to form a paste. Season the rib roast with salt and pepper. Rub the paste all over the rib roast and place into a roasting pan with the bones resting on the bottom of the pan.

Roast for 15 minutes. Reduce the temperature to 325°F and continue roasting until the rib roast is cooked to your liking. For medium-rare meat (center is very pink) roast until the internal temperature is 130°F, approximately 15 minutes per pound. For medium cooked meat (where the center is slightly pink), the internal temperature should be 140°F. Medium well done (no pink) is at 150°F, and well done meat is 160°F.

Remove the rib roast and let rest at least 10 minutes before carving. If you wish, make gravy from the defatted pan drippings during this time. Cut through and separate the rib bones and serve separately like spareribs.

Zucchini Tomato Onion Gratin

SERVES 8 TO 10 *This versatile side dish goes especially well with holiday roasts or grilled meats. It can be made and assembled the day before, then baked just before serving.*

2 tablespoons olive oil

2 cups sliced onions

1 tablespoon brown sugar

3 zucchini (approximately 18 ounces total weight)

½ teaspoon salt

¼ teaspoon pepper

Topping

1 cup Panko bread crumbs

⅓ cup grated parmesan cheese

¼ cup olive oil

½ teaspoon salt

¼ teaspoon pepper

¼ teaspoon garlic powder

¼ cup basil, finely chopped

3 Beefsteak tomatoes, sliced ⅓-inch-thick

Heat a 12-inch skillet and add the olive oil. Turn the heat to low, add the sliced onions, and sauté for approximately 12 minutes, turning frequently until the onions are soft and just starting to brown. A few minutes before they are done, stir in the brown sugar and continue cooking. Remove onions from the skillet and set aside.

Cut the unpeeled zucchini crosswise into ¼-inch-thick rounds. (You should end up with approximately 4 cups). Add more oil to the pan to lightly cover the bottom, and add the zucchini, salt and pepper. Sauté for 5 minutes, stirring and turning them occasionally, until they are just starting to get tender.

Preheat oven to 400°F.

TO MAKE THE TOPPING: In a bowl, mix together the Panko, parmesan cheese, olive oil, salt, pepper, garlic powder, and basil.

Spray a 2-quart rectangular casserole or 3-quart shallow gratin dish with vegetable spray. Add the cooked zucchini and spread out evenly. Top with the cooked onions, and the tomato slices. Sprinkle the Panko Topping over the top.

Bake for 20 minutes, then cover the bread crumbs with aluminum foil to keep from burning. Continue cooking for another 20 minutes.

Individual Baked Alaska

By Emily Luchetti. Adapted from *A Passion for Ice Cream*, (Chronicle Books 2005).

SERVES 8 *This version of baked Alaska has a rich, fudge-like brownie base which is topped with peppermint ice cream and a traditional meringue. It requires a blow torch, a relatively inexpensive and handy gadget to have in the kitchen for crème brûlées and meringues.*

Brownies

8 ounces bittersweet chocolate, finely chopped

1 ounce unsweetened chocolate, finely chopped

5 ounces (10 tablespoons) unsalted butter

½ cup all-purpose flour

⅛ teaspoon kosher salt

½ teaspoon baking powder

3 tablespoons unsweetened cocoa powder

3 large eggs

1¼ cups sugar

Meringue

8 scoops peppermint or coffee ice cream

½ cup egg whites (about 4)

1 cup sugar

TO MAKE THE BROWNIES: Preheat the oven to 350°F. Grease the bottom of a 9-by-13-inch baking pan and line it with parchment paper.

Melt the bittersweet and unsweetened chocolates and the butter in a double boiler over hot water, just until melted. Set aside to cool In a bowl, whisk together the flour, salt, baking powder, and cocoa powder.

In the bowl of a KitchenAid stand mixer, beat the eggs and sugar until well incorporated Continue mixing and slowly pour in the melted chocolate mixture. Turn the speed to low, add the dry ingredients and mix just until blended. Spread the batter into the prepared pan.

Bake until a skewer inserted in the center comes out fudge-like and not dry, about 20 minutes. Let cool to room temperature. Run a knife around the inside edge of the pan. Place a cutting board on top of the pan. Invert the pan and cutting board. Remove the pan and carefully peel off the parchment paper. With a glass or round cutter, cut the brownies into eight 2½-inch rounds.

TO MAKE THE MERINGUE AND ASSEMBLE THE BAKED ALASKA: Place the cake rounds on a baking sheet. Place a scoop of ice cream on each, making sure to leave a little more than a ¼-inch border of cake around the ice cream. Freeze the cakes for 1 hour or up to overnight. If freezing overnight, cover with plastic wrap.

In the bowl of a KitchenAid stand mixer, whisk together the egg whites and sugar until combined. Put the bowl in a saucepan of simmering water and whisk constantly until the egg whites are very warm. Remove the bowl from the hot water and place it on the KitchenAid stand mixer fitted with a wire whip. Turn on medium-high speed (or high speed if using a handheld mixer), until stiff, glossy peaks form and the mixture has cooled to room temperature.

Remove the cakes from the freezer. Using a small spatula, spread the meringue over the ice cream, completely covering it but leaving the cake edges exposed. If desired, this can be done several hours in advance. Do not cover. Freeze until ready to serve.

When ready to serve, brown the meringue with a propane or butane torch by constantly moving the flame over the meringue until golden brown.

Using a large metal spatula, transfer the Baked Alaska from the sheet pan onto individual plates. Serve immediately,

Zabaglione Filled Pannetone

SERVES 16 *Zabaglione, a custard-like dessert with a light, creamy and fluffy texture, is considered by some to be one of the greatest gifts the Italians gave to the world. In this recipe, Emily Luchetti, co-host of* The Holiday Table *television series, fills a hollowed out pannetone with this luscious treat, creating the ultimate holiday treat.*

> One, 2½ pound pannetone (8½ inches wide)
> 6 large egg yolks
> 6 tablespoons sugar
> ½ cup Marsala
> Salt
> 1½ cups heavy whipping cream
> 1¼ cups chocolate chips

Cut a 5½-inch circle in the middle top of the pannetone. Hollow out ⅔ of the center of the pannetone.

Whisk together the egg yolks, sugar, Marsala, and salt in the bowl of a KitchenAid stand mixer. Place the bowl over a pot of boiling water, making sure the water is not touching the bottom of the bowl. Whisk continually by hand until it is thick, like mayonnaise, about 3 minutes. Place the bowl over an ice bath and cool to room temperature.

Attach the bowl to the KitchenAid stand mixer fitted with the wire whip attachment. Whip the heavy cream to soft peaks. Remove from the mixer, and fold the whipped cream and the chocolate chips into the Marsala mixture.

Fill the inside of the Pannetone with the zabaglione cream. Cover with plastic wrap and refrigerate for one hour or overnight.

Slice and serve.

VARIATION: QUICK AND EASY VERSION

SERVES 6 TO 8

Cut a 3½-inch circle in the middle of the top of a 1-pound Pannetone. Hollow out ⅔ of the center of the Pannetone.

In the bowl of a KitchenAid stand mixer, using the wire whip attachment, whip 1 cup cream with 1 tablespoon of sugar, the grated zest from one orange, and ¼ teaspoon vanilla extract until it forms soft peaks. Fold in ¾ cup chocolate chips. Fill and serve as directed above.

Lord Wedgwood Christmas Fruitcake

Lord Piers Wedgwood, 8th generation descendant of the famous china family, generously shared this recipe for his family's Christmas fruitcake which has been a family favorite for many generations. With a healthy dose of brandy and dried fruit, it has a delicious, rich flavor.

5 cups currants

5 cups golden raisins

1 cup brandy plus more for brushing
    the top of the cake if desired

8 tablespoons (1 stick) cold unsalted butter

5⅓ cups all-purpose flour

1 cup brown sugar

⅓ cup ground toasted almonds

Grated zest from one lemon

3 large eggs, lightly beaten

1 tablespoon molasses or treacle

1 cup milk

2 tablespoons lemon juice

Preheat the oven to 325°F. Grease the bottom and sides of a 9-inch spring form pan.

In a large bowl, mix together the currants, golden raisins and ½ cup of the brandy.

In the bowl of a KitchenAid stand mixer, mix the butter with the flour on medium low speed until the mixture resembles small peas. Add the sugar, ground almonds and grated lemon zest. Mix until just combined.

In a separate bowl, whisk together the eggs, molasses, milk, lemon juice and remaining ½ cup brandy. Add it to the flour and butter mixture and mix. When it is about half combined, add the currants and golden raisins and mix until just combined. The batter will be very stiff.

Spread the batter into the prepared pan. Bake for 1½ hours.

Cool completely before removing the spring form from the pan. Brush the top with more brandy if desired. Wrap well in plastic wrap. This cake will keep for some time.

Christmas
Cookie
Exchange

Classic Rolled Sugar Cookies

Excerpted from *A Baker's Field Guide to Christmas Cookies*, by Dede Wilson. © 2006, used by permission from The Harvard Common Press.

MAKES 36 THREE-INCH COOKIES

3¾ cups all-purpose flour

½ teaspoon salt

1½ cups (3 sticks) unsalted butter, at room temperature, cut into tablespoon-sized pieces

1½ cups sugar, plus more for decorating

1½ teaspoons vanilla extract

3 large eggs

Colored sugars

Whisk the flour and salt together in a small bowl. Set aside.

Place the butter in the bowl of a KitchenAid stand mixer and beat using the flat paddle on medium-high speed until creamy, about 2 minutes. Gradually add the sugar and continue beating, scraping down the bowl once or twice, until light and fluffy, about 3 minutes. Add the vanilla extract and the eggs one at a time, beating well after each addition, and scraping down the bowl once or twice.

With the stand mixer off, add about ⅓ of the flour, then beat on low-speed. Gradually add the remaining flour, scraping down the bowl once or twice, and mixing until just blended. Form into two very flat discs, wrap in plastic wrap, and refrigerate at least 2 hours or until firm enough to roll. Dough may be refrigerated overnight. (You may freeze dough up to 1 month. Defrost in refrigerator overnight before proceeding).

Preheat oven to 350°F. Line two cookie sheets with parchment paper.

On a floured work surface, roll out one of the chilled discs to ¼-inch-thick. You may need to flour your rolling pin, too. Cut out cookies using your choice of cookie cutters. Transfer the cookies to the prepared cookie sheets at least 2 inches apart.

Decorate with colored sugars or regular sugar in decorative patterns.

Bake for about 10 minutes or until the edges begin to turn a light golden brown. Slide the parchment with the cookies onto wire racks and cool completely. They can be stored at room temperature, tightly wrapped, for about 1 month.

Iced Sugar Cookies

Excerpted from *A Baker's Field Guide to Christmas Cookies*, by Dede Wilson. © 2006, used by permission from The Harvard Common Press.

MAKES 36 THREE-INCH COOKIES *In this sugar cookie recipe the decoration is provided by Royal Icing which is applied after the cookies have cooled. Thick icing is used for making outlines, a medium texture is used for embellishments on already dry icing and the thin version is used to flood the thick outlines to cover cookies completely.*

1 Recipe Classic Rolled Sugar Cookies (page 97)

Thick Royal Icing (see Note)

3¾ cups powdered sugar, sifted

3 large egg whites

Gel, paste, liquid or powdered food coloring

Medium Royal Icing (see Note)

3¾ cups powdered sugar, sifted

3 large egg whites

1 tablespoon water

Gel, paste, liquid or powdered food coloring

Thin Royal Icing (see Note)

3¾ cups powdered sugar, sifted

3 large egg whites

2 tablespoons water

Gel, paste, liquid or powdered food coloring

Bake Classic Rolled Sugar Cookies as directed and let cool completely before decorating.

TO MAKE ROYAL ICING: Place the powdered sugar, egg whites, and water, if using, in the bowl of a KitchenAid stand mixer. Using the whisk attachment, whip on high speed until thick and creamy, about 6 minutes. Tint with gel, paste or liquid food coloring, if desired (powdered colors are dusted over dry icing). Use a toothpick to pick up small amounts of color; you can always add more.

Spoon Thick Royal Icing into a pastry bag fitted with a coupler and a very small round tip (such as Ateco #2) and pipe an outline around the edge of the cookie, or define a section you want to cover with icing. Make sure to create a solid line all the way around. Allow to dry. To fill the outlined section use Thin Royal Icing, use the small round tip and allow the icing to flow into the outlined area. After the icing dries the cookie will be completely covered with a smooth layer of icing, which will dry hard. To embellish the cookie with details, such as eyes or clothing or whatever else you like, use the Medium Royal Icing on the dry cookie. Cookies may be stored at room temperature in an airtight container for up to 1 month. These cookies are best stored in single layers separated by waxed paper or parchment paper.

Note: Thick Royal Icing is used to pipe a complete border around the cookies' edges. A dab of thick icing will be stiff enough to hold a peak.

Medium Royal Icing can be used to create three-dimensional effects to already dry icing (such as adding eyes to an already iced cookie). A dab of medium textured icing will puddle slightly and form a thick, dimensional circle.

Thin Royal Icing is used to cover cookies completely, or to cover partial sections that have been outlined with a thick textured border. Two colors (or more) of thin icing can be swirled together to create a marbled effect.

Painted Sugar Cookies

Excerpted from *A Baker's Field Guide to Christmas Cookies*, by Dede Wilson. © 2006, used by permission from The Harvard Common Press.

MAKES 36 THREE-INCH COOKIES *Using the basic sugar cookie dough, you can also decorate them with edible "paint" as opposed to sugar or icing. It is very easy to make using just two ingredients, egg yolk and food coloring. The paint is applied before baking, so you do not have to worry about raw eggs.*

1 Recipe Classic Rolled Sugar Cookies (page 97)

Edible Paint

4 large egg yolks

Gel, paste or liquid food coloring

Soft artist's brush

Roll out and cut cookies as directed in the recipe for Classic Rolled Sugar Cookies. Transfer the cookies to the prepared cookie sheets, placing them at least 2 inches apart. Set aside.

TO MAKE THE EDIBLE PAINT: In a small bowl, whisk the egg yolks until loosened and smooth. Divide the yolk into as many small bowls as you want colors. Tint each batch with the color of your choice, stirring in tiny bits of color at a time (you can always add more). Stir until the color is well mixed with the yolk.

Use a soft artist's brush to paint the cookies with Edible Paint as desired.

Bake, cool, and store as directed in the main recipe for Classic Rolled Sugar Cookies.

Almond Kisses

MAKES 36 COOKIES *These light, sweet, and crisp meringue cookies are truly ambrosial, especially with their delicious almond accents. When whipping egg whites, be sure your bowl and beaters are absolutely clean and free of moisture or grease. Also, it is best to beat egg whites when they are at room temperature to get maximum volume.*

3 egg whites, at room temperature

1½ cups sugar

1 teaspoon almond extract

2 cups sliced almonds

Preheat oven to 325°F. Grease and flour 2 baking sheets or cover them with parchment paper.

Using the KitchenAid stand mixer fitted with a wire whip, place egg whites in mixer bowl. Whip for approximately 2 minutes at high speed, or until soft peaks form.

Reduce to medium speed and gradually add the sugar, beating for about 1 minute. Stop and scrape the bowl. Add the almond extract. Turn to high speed and whip 1½ minutes more, or until the mixture very stiff. Fold in the almonds with rubber spatula.

Drop by tablespoonfuls onto the prepared pans. Bake for 15 minutes. Cool on wire racks.

Kris Kringle's Chocolate Krinkles

Excerpted from *A Baker's Field Guide to Christmas Cookies*, by Dede Wilson. © 2006, used by permission from The Harvard Common Press.

MAKES 80 COOKIES *These chocolate cookies with their slightly cracked exterior and chewy, rich interior are a holiday favorite. They may be stored at room temperature in an airtight container for up to 2 weeks. For best results, use a high quality chocolate.*

> 5 ounces unsweetened chocolate, finely chopped
> ½ cup (1 stick) unsalted butter, cut into tablespoon-sized pieces
> 2 cups all-purpose flour
> 2 teaspoons baking powder
> ¼ teaspoon salt
> 4 large eggs
> 2 cups sugar
> 1 teaspoon vanilla extract
> Powdered sugar
> Cocoa powder

Melt the chocolate and butter together in top of a double boiler or in the microwave until about three-quarters of the way melted. Remove from double boiler or microwave and stir until completely melted and smooth.

Stir together the flour, baking powder and salt. Set aside.

Place the eggs, sugar, and vanilla extract in the work bowl of a KitchenAid stand mixer and, using the wire whip attachment, whip on high speed until creamy, about 2 minutes.

Using the paddle attachment, beat the chocolate-butter mixture into to the egg mixture until smooth, scraping down the bowl once or twice.

With the stand mixer off, add about one-third of the flour mixture to the bowl, then mix at low-speed. Gradually add the remaining flour, mixing until just blended, scraping down bowl once or twice. The dough may seem very thin. It will firm up as it cools. Cover with plastic wrap and refrigerate at least 6 hours or overnight or until the dough is firm enough to roll.

Preheat oven to 350°F. Line two cookie sheets with parchment paper.

Sift some powdered sugar into a small bowl and set aside. Sift some cocoa into a small bowl and set aside.

Roll a small amount of dough between your palms to make a 1-inch ball. Roll it in the powdered sugar or the cocoa and coat it completely Place the ball on a prepared cookie sheet and repeat with the remaining dough, making sure the balls are at least 2-inches apart. Gently flatten each ball just enough so they don't roll off the sheet.

Bake for about 12 minutes or until the ball has a puffed, crackled appearance, and the surface is dry to the touch. The centers will be somewhat soft. You should be able to gently lift the edge of a cookie up from the sheet with a spatula. Slide the parchment with the cookies onto wire racks and cool completely.

Ginger Sandwich Cookies with Mascarpone Filling

By Emily Luchetti. Adapted from *Classic Stars Desserts* (Chronicle, 2007).

MAKES ABOUT 30 COOKIES *These cookies bring ginger cookies to a festive new level with a creamy, brandy-flavored Mascarpone filling and chocolate drizzled on top.*

Cookies

2¼ cups all-purpose flour

2 teaspoons baking soda

2 teaspoons ground ginger

1 teaspoon ground cinnamon

½ teaspoon ground allspice

½ teaspoon kosher salt

¼ teaspoon ground white pepper

¾ cup granulated sugar

½ cup firmly packed light brown sugar

16 tablespoons (2 sticks) unsalted butter, at room temperature

1 large egg

⅓ cup light or dark molasses

Filling

1½ cups mascarpone cheese

1½ tablespoons granulated sugar

½ teaspoon vanilla extract

Nutmeg

2 teaspoons brandy

Melted chocolate for drizzling (optional)

In a bowl, stir together the flour, baking soda, ginger, cinnamon, allspice, salt, and pepper. Set aside.

Combine ½ cup of the granulated sugar, the brown sugar, and the butter in the bowl of a KitchenAid stand mixer fitted with the paddle attachment and beat on medium speed until smooth, about 1 minute. Add the egg and beat until mixed, and then beat in the molasses until blended. Reduce the speed to low, slowly add the dry ingredients, and mix until incorporated. Refrigerate the dough for 30 minutes.

Preheat the oven to 325°F. Line 2 baking sheets with parchment paper.

Spread the remaining ¼ cup granulated sugar in a small, shallow bowl. To shape each cookie, use a small spoon or ice cream scoop to scoop up a spoonful of the dough and roll between your palms into a ¾-inch ball. As the balls are formed, roll them in the sugar, coating evenly, and place them on the prepared baking sheets, spacing them 2 to 3 inches apart. Flatten the balls slightly with 2 fingers.

Bake until golden brown and set around the edges but still soft inside, about 12 minutes. At the midway point, switch the pans between the racks and rotate them 180°F to ensure even baking. Let cool on the pans to room temperature.

TO MAKE THE FILLING: In a bowl, mix together the mascarpone cheese, sugar, vanilla extract, a big pinch of nutmeg, and the brandy until well combined. Spread the filling on the flat edge of one cookie and then top with a second cookie to make a sandwich.

If you like, melt some chocolate and spoon into a sturdy, self-sealing plastic bag. Snip a tiny corner of the bag and drizzle chocolate in lines over the cookie sandwiches.

The dough may be made up to a week in advance and kept in the refrigerator. The cookies may be baked a day ahead. Store in an airtight container at room temperature.

Menage a Trois Cookies

Excerpted from *A Baker's Field Guide to Chocolate Chip Cookies* by Dede Wilson. © 2004, used by permission from The Harvard Common Press.

MAKES 28 COOKIES *Packed with white, milk and dark chocolate chunks, these creamy, truffle-like, dark chocolate cookies are best eaten within a day or two when their texture is at their best. These are the ultimate chocolate cookie and give you as much of a buzz as a small cup of coffee.*

¼ **cup all-purpose flour**

¼ **teaspoon baking powder**

½ **teaspoon salt**

6 **ounces semisweet chocolate, finely chopped**

2 **ounces unsweetened chocolate, finely chopped**

6 **tablespoons (¾ stick) unsalted butter, at room temperature, cut into tablespoon-sized pieces**

¾ **cup granulated sugar**

2 **large eggs**

1½ **teaspoons vanilla extract**

2 **cups semisweet or bittersweet chocolate chunks (½-inch size)**

¾ **cup milk chocolate chunks (½-inch size)**

¾ **cup white chocolate chunks (½-inch size)**

Preheat the oven to 350°F. Line 2 cookie sheets with parchment paper.

Whisk the flour, baking powder, and salt together in a small bowl. Set aside.

Melt the semisweet and unsweetened chocolates together with the butter in the top of a double boiler or in the microwave. Stir occasionally until smooth. Cool slightly to nearly room temperature.

Place the sugar, eggs, and vanilla in the work bowl of a KitchenAid stand mixer and beat on high-speed using the whisk attachment. Beat until light and fluffy, 2 to 5 minutes. Gently fold in the chocolate-butter mixture and beat until no chocolate streaks remain. Slowly pour the flour mixture into the batter and mix until just combined.

Toss the three kinds of chocolate chunks together in a bowl and set aside about one-quarter of them in a separate bowl. Fold the large portion of the chocolate chunks into the batter. Drop the batter by generously rounded tablespoon onto the cookie sheet, making sure to place them at least 2 inches apart. Press chunks of the reserved chocolate pieces into each cookie. (When baked, the white chocolate, milk chocolate, and dark chocolate colors will look beautiful.)

Bake for about 10 minutes, or until tops look and feel dry but the insides are still soft and creamy. The edges will be slightly firmer than the rest of the cookies. They firm up tremendously upon cooling; do not over bake. Place the cookie sheets on wire racks to cool the cookies for 1 minute, then slide the parchment with the cookies directly onto the wire racks and let them cool completely.

Store for 2 days in an airtight container at room temperature.

Cranberry Almond Biscotti

MAKES 36 COOKIES *Biscotti, an Italian term referring to "twice-baked" cookies, are the perfect accompaniment to coffee and also make a great holiday gift. If you prefer a chocolate variation, substitute mini chocolate chips for the cranberries and coffee for the orange juice.*

¼ cup vegetable oil

1½ cups lightly packed brown sugar

2 eggs

¼ cup orange juice

1 teaspoon vanilla extract

2½ cups all-purpose flour

1 cup old fashioned rolled oats, finely ground

1½ teaspoons baking powder

½ teaspoon salt

½ cup blanched slivered almonds, toasted

¾ cup dried cranberries

Preheat oven to 375°F. Lightly grease a non-stick baking sheet

Using a KitchenAid stand mixer with the paddle attachment, beat the oil, brown sugar, eggs, orange juice, and vanilla extract together until smooth. In a separate bowl, mix together the flour, rolled oats, baking powder, and salt.

Slowly add the flour mixture to the wet mixture, beating on low speed until smooth. Using a wooden spoon, fold in the almonds and the cranberries.

Divide the dough in half and shape into two logs. Transfer to the prepared baking sheet, making sure to place the logs at least 2 inches apart. Bake for 25 minutes.

Remove the cookies from the oven and lower the temperature to 350°F. Let the cookies cool for 10 minutes.

Slice the cookies and return them to the baking sheet. Bake for 20 minutes, or until browned.

Russian Tea Cookies

MAKES 18 COOKIES *Also called Mexican wedding cookies, these pecan-studded balls smothered in powdered sugar are a wonderful holiday tradition in many homes. In planning your cookie platters, they make a nice contrast to chocolate cookies.*

- 1 cup pecans
- 1 cup softened butter or margarine
- ¾ cup powdered sugar
- 2 teaspoons vanilla
- ¼ teaspoon salt
- 2¼ cups all-purpose flour

Preheat the oven to 350°F.

Place the pecans on a baking sheet in a single layer. Place into the oven and bake for 8 to 10 minutes until the pecans are slightly browned and aromatic. Let cool, then place in the bowl of food processor and chop until fine.

Reduce the oven to 325°F. In the work bowl of a KitchenAid stand mixer, mix together the butter, sugar, and vanilla on low speed until well combined, about 1 minute. Gradually add the salt and the flour and beat until just combined. Using a wooden spoon stir in the toasted pecans.

Using your hands, take a small portion of dough and roll it into a 1-inch ball. Place the ball on an ungreased cookie sheet and repeat with the rest of the dough, making sure to place them at least 1 inch apart.

Bake at 325°F for 10 to 12 minutes until firm to the touch but not browned. Do not over bake.

While still warm, roll each cookie in powdered sugar and set on a wire rack to cool completely. Just before serving, roll the cookies in powdered sugar one more time.

Candy Cane Delights

MAKES 44 COOKIES *These peppermint flavored cookies are mixed with speckles of candy canes, making them as pretty as they are delicious. Note they cook at a lower temperature and longer period of time than regular cookies which allows the bits of candy cane to stay crisp for an extra bit of crunch.*

- 2 cups unsalted butter, softened
- 1 cup sugar
- 1 teaspoon peppermint extract
- 3½ cups all-purpose flour
- 1 cup rice flour
- ¾ cup crushed candy canes

Preheat oven to 275°F.

In the bowl of a KitchenAid stand mixer with the paddle attachment, beat the butter until it turns almost white. Add the sugar and peppermint extract and continue to beat until fluffy.

In a separate bowl, stir together the all-purpose flour and the rice flour. Add it to butter mixture in 3 additions, beating on low. Stir in the crushed candy canes by hand.

Gather the dough together and divide into 4 discs. Roll each disk between 2 pieces of parchment paper to a ¼-inch thickness. Cut out cookies using a 3-inch round cookie cutter (or shape of your choice) Place on a parchment paper lined baking sheet. Freeze for 15 minutes or until firm. Repeat with the remaining dough, re-rolling the scraps as needed.

Bake for 30 minutes, or until firm, and let cool on the baking sheet for 5 minutes. Transfer the rounds to wire racks and cool completely.

Kwaanza

Benne (Sesame Seed) Wafers

MAKES 60 COOKIES *These crispy and delightful sesame cookies have become a tradition at Kwaanza as a reminder that sesame seeds came to America during the African slave trade. Benne, the Bantu word for sesame, are thought to bring good luck.*

1 cup sesame seeds

1 cup all-purpose flour

¼ teaspoon baking soda

¼ teaspoon salt

6 tablespoons butter, softened

1 cup packed brown sugar

1 egg

1 teaspoon vanilla extract

Preheat oven to 375°F. Grease cookie sheets or line with parchment paper.

Spread the sesame seeds on a sheet pan and place in the oven for 8 to 10 minutes until toasty and aromatic. Watch carefully so they do not burn.

Whisk together the flour, baking soda, and salt. In the bowl of a KitchenAid stand mixer with the paddle attachment, cream together the butter and sugar. Add the egg and vanilla and beat until well blended. Reduce the speed to low, and slowly add the dry ingredients just until incorporated.

Drop by small teaspoonfuls onto the cookie sheet approximately 2 inches apart. Bake for 6 to 8 minutes until the cookies are light brown. Allow to cool for 2 minutes, then remove from the sheet pan and let cool on a wire rack.

Okra, Corn & Tomato Sauté

SERVES 4 TO 6 *The vegetable okra came to America by way of African slaves who turned it into a popular Southern ingredient, often found in gumbo and stews because of its natural thickening agent. If you can't find it fresh, it is widely available frozen.*

1½ pounds fresh okra

3 slices bacon, cut into ¼-inch pieces

2 cloves garlic, finely chopped

½ cup chopped onion

1 can (14 ounces) diced tomatoes

1 teaspoon salt

Freshly ground black pepper

1 teaspoon hot sauce, or more as needed

1 teaspoon Worcestershire sauce

1½ cup frozen corn

Wash the okra and trim the ends, as needed.

In a large sauté pan, cook the bacon pieces until the fat has rendered and the bacon is crisp. Transfer the bacon to a paper towel-lined plate and set aside.

Add the garlic and onions to the sauté pan and cook 3 minutes, until soft. Add the okra and cook sauté for 5 minutes. Add the tomatoes, salt, pepper, hot sauce, Worcestershire sauce and the corn. Stir to mix well and cover. Simmer over low heat for 10 to 15 minutes more. Add the bacon pieces, check the seasonings, adding more salt or hot sauce if necessary. Serve.

Gulf Coast Gumbo

By Joyce White, food writer and author of *Soul Food* and *Brown Sugar* (published by HarperCollins)

SERVES 8 TO 10 *This legendary Southern dish is a deep, rich stew that contains a variety of meat and fish bound together by a thickening agent called a roux. The passion for gumbo is so deep in the South that contests are held regularly to ferret out the best Gumbo cooks. This recipe by Joyce White can compete among the best.*

½ cup peanut oil or corn oil

3 pounds chicken thighs and legs

½ pound smoked sausage or ham, cut into one-inch cubes (optional)

2 large red or green bell peppers, or one of each, seeded and chopped

1 large yellow onion, sliced

2 celery ribs, diced

3 to 4 cloves garlic, crushed

¼ cup chopped fresh parsley or fresh basil

1 teaspoon red pepper flakes, plus more if needed

1 tablespoon chopped fresh thyme or 1½ teaspoons dried thyme, crushed

½ cup all-purpose flour

One 14-ounce can diced tomatoes with their juice

4 bay leaves

1 tablespoon salt

Freshly ground black pepper

5 to 6 cups hot Fish Stock (recipe follows)

Two 10-ounce packages frozen whole okra (see Note)

2 pounds medium-sized shrimp, shelled (see Note)

2 to 3 cups shucked oysters

1 to 2 tablespoons gumbo file (optional)

½ to 1 pound crabmeat

Using a large heavy pot (at least 6 quarts), heat ¼ cup of the oil. Add 3 or 4 pieces of chicken to the pot and brown on all sides, turning frequently, 8 to 10 minutes. Transfer the chicken to a platter and continue browning the remaining pieces the same way.

Reduce the heat to medium low and stir in the sausage or ham (if using), bell peppers, onion, celery, garlic, parsley or basil, red pepper flakes, and thyme. Cook until the onions are soft and translucent and the bell pepper is tender, about 8 minutes. Transfer to a bowl and set aside.

To make a roux, add the remaining ¼ cup oil to the pot and briskly stir in the flour using a wire whisk. Cook the flour mixture over medium-low heat for 10 to 12 minutes, whisking constantly, until the flour turns the shade of a walnut or peanut. Watch carefully to prevent the flour from burning.

Return the sausage or ham (if using) and the vegetables back to the pot. Stir in the tomatoes along with their juices, the bay leaves, salt, and pepper to taste.

Turn the heat up and bring to a boil, stirring briskly and breaking up the tomatoes into small pieces with a large spoon, and continue cooking over high heat for 3 or 4 more minutes.

Reduce the heat to low and let the sauce cook uncovered 30 minutes longer, stirring occasionally.

Add the hot fish stock to the pot, stirring until well combined, then add the browned chicken. If the sauce is bubbling, reduce the heat a bit. Cook, uncovered, stirring occasionally, for 40 minutes to 1 hour or until the liquid thickens to the consistency of thick maple syrup.

Add the okra and cook for about 5 minutes or until tender, but not gooey. Add the shrimp and oysters and cook, stirring gently from time to time, over low heat for 10 to 15 minutes, or until the shrimp are pink and tender.

Taste the gumbo and add more seasoning if needed. Add the gumbo file (if using). Stir in the crabmeat and heat thoroughly. If you prefer the gumbo thinner, heat a cup or so of the remaining fish stock and stir into the pot.

Note: If available, fresh okra can also be used. Cook the okra for about 10 minutes before adding the seafood.

Use the shrimp shells to make fish stock (recipe follows)

Fish Stock

Shells from two pounds medium-size shrimp

1 onion, sliced

1 bay leaf

½ teaspoon peppercorns

2 celery ribs, cut into 1-inch pieces

Rinse the shrimp shells thoroughly, drain, and place in a 3-quart pot. Add the onion, bay leaf, peppercorns, and celery. Add 7 cups of water. Turn the heat to high and bring to a boil. Cover, reduce the heat to low, and simmer for 30 minutes. Pour stock through a fine-mesh sieve and discard the solids.

· ·

Sweet Potato Fries

By Joyce White, food writer and author of *Soul Food* and *Brown Sugar* (published by HarperCollins)

SERVES 4 *Sweet potato fries are quickly working their way into restaurant menus all over the country as people discover their sweet and crunchy goodness. They're easy to make at home, but be sure the oil is at the right temperature. If it's too low, the fries will get soggy. Too hot, and they'll burn.*

> 4 yams or sweet potatoes with orange flesh
>
> 1 teaspoon salt
>
> 3 cups cooking oil
>
> Sea salt or a mixture of spices such as allspice, cinnamon and cayenne

Scrub and rinse the potatoes. Cut away any blemishes or sprouts. Peel the potatoes and cut into ½-inch-thick slices lengthwise. Cut again lengthwise into strips to make French fries. (You can leave the potatoes unpeeled if desired.) Fill a large bowl with ice cubes and water. Add the salt and stir to combine. Add the cut up potatoes and let soak for at least 30 minutes. Drain and pat dry with paper towels.

Heat the oil in a deep heavy pot or skillet until it reaches 365°F on a deep-fry thermometer. Add a handful of the potatoes to the hot oil and cook for 4 or 5 minutes, until golden brown and tender, turning over with long-handled tongs as they fry.

Remove the potatoes from the oil, drain on paper towels, and keep warm in a 250°F oven. Repeat with the rest of the potatoes.

Sprinkle lightly with the salt or a spice mixture before serving (if desired).

VARIATION:

For oven-roasted sweet potatoes, preheat the oven to 400°F. Cut the potatoes into strips or spears about 1-inch wide. Pour the oil into a skillet or roasting pan and heat in the oven, on a lower shelf, for about 5 minutes, or until very hot. Remove the pan from the oven and add the potatoes to the pan, trying not to crowd them or the potatoes will steam instead of roast.

Roast the potatoes about 20 minutes, turn over with a metal spatula, and roast for another 15 to 20 minutes, or until they are golden all over and the edges are browned. Watch carefully to be sure they don't burn. Toss the potatoes with a little coarse salt if desired, and keep warm until serving.

African Vegetable Pot Pie

SERVES 6 TO 8 *Yams and peanuts are the central ingredients in this colorful and savory vegetarian pot pie. It's a perfect choice for a Kwaanza celebration.*

1 tablespoon olive oil

1 onion, chopped (about 1 cup)

1 garlic clove, chopped

1½ bunches Swiss chard, center ribs discarded and coarsely chopped

1 can garbanzo beans, drained

½ cup raisins

2 small yams, (8 ounces) diced ¼-inch-cubes

One 14 ounce can diced tomatoes, drained of half the liquid

1 teaspoon salt

¼ teaspoon red pepper flakes

¼ teaspoon black pepper

¼ cup coarsely chopped peanuts

2 cups rice, cooked

1 puff pastry sheet, thawed

1 egg

1 tablespoon water

Preheat the oven to 400°F.

Heat a large sauté pan or 4- to 5- quart soup pot and add the olive oil. Over medium heat, add the onion and sauté until soft, 3 to 4 minutes. Add garlic and Swiss chard and continue cooking until the chard is tender. Add the garbanzos, raisins, yams, tomatoes, salt, red pepper flakes, and black pepper. Cover and simmer for 10 minutes. Stir in the chopped peanuts.

Line the bottom of a 10-inch deep-dish pie pan with the cooked rice. Spoon the vegetable mixture over the rice. Roll out the puff pastry on a lightly floured surface big enough to fit over the top of the pan. Mix together the egg and water and brush over the puff pastry. (If you like, cut decorative shapes from the scraps of puff pastry and place on top of the pie.) Cut some small vents or a 1-inch hole in the middle of the pastry to allow steam to escape.

Transfer the pan to the oven and cook for approximately 20 minutes until golden brown.

Buttermilk Ginger Cake

By Joyce White, food writer and author of *Soul Food* and *Brown Sugar* (published by HarperCollins)

SERVES 8 TO 10 *The punch of fresh ginger combined with the silky richness of butter-milk makes this a moist and temptingly fragrant cake.*

2 cups all-purpose flour

¼ teaspoon salt

1 teaspoon baking powder

¾ teaspoon baking soda

1½ teaspoons nutmeg

One 3-inch piece fresh ginger (see Note)

1¼ cups sugar

12 tablespoons (1½ sticks) unsalted butter, softened

3 large eggs, at room temperature

1 teaspoon pure vanilla extract

1 cup buttermilk, at room temperature

Preheat oven to 350°F. Generously butter and flour a 9-by-2-inch round cake pan.

In a medium bowl, sift together the flour, salt, baking powder, baking soda, and nutmeg. Peel the ginger, making sure to trim away and discard any woody parts. In the bowl of a KitchenAid food processor fitted with the multipurpose blade, chop the ginger with 2 table-spoons of the sugar until very fine.

Combine the ginger, remaining sugar, and the butter in the bowl of a KitchenAid stand mixer fitted with the paddle attachment. Beat the mixture at medium-high speed until pale and fluffy, 3 to 5 minutes, stopping and scraping the bowl with a rubber spatula two or three times. Add the eggs, one at a time, and beat 30 seconds after each addition. Add the vanilla extract and beat well. Reduce the mixer to low speed. Slowly add the flour mixture, adding alternately with the buttermilk and mixing only for a few seconds until blended.

After the last addition, beat the batter on low speed for 30 seconds, scraping the bowl as needed. If the batter is a little thick, add a little more buttermilk and stir to mix well.

Pour the batter into the prepared pan and spread the top evenly with a spatula. Shake the pan gently to settle the batter. Place the cake on the lower oven rack and bake for 45 to 50 minutes, or until a cake tester or toothpick inserted in the center comes out clean.

Transfer the cake to a wire rack and cool in the pan for 10 minutes. Run a metal spatula around the inside edge of the pan and invert the pan onto the rack, tap gently, and remove the pan. Place the cake, top side up, on the rack and cool completely.

Note: Two generous teaspoons of ground ginger can replace the fresh ginger root, if unavailable.

Chocolate for the Holidays

Drunken Chocolate Cake

By Emily Luchetti. Reprinted with permission from *Classic Stars Desserts* (Chronicle Books 2007).

SERVES 8 TO 10 *Here's a sweet moist chocolate cake laced with rum and topped with a simple chocolate glaze. The whipped egg whites give the cake an airy quality.*

Chocolate Cake
4½ ounces bittersweet chocolate, coarsely chopped

3 ounces (6 tablespoons) unsalted butter

½ cup dark rum

3 large eggs, separated

½ cup plus ⅓ cup sugar

¾ cup all-purpose flour

Kosher salt

Chocolate Glaze
¾ cup heavy whipping cream

6 ounces bittersweet chocolate, coarsely chopped

Chantilly Cream (recipe follows)

TO MAKE THE CHOCOLATE CAKE: Preheat the oven to 350°F. Line the bottom of a 9-inch round cake pan with parchment paper.

Melt the chocolate, butter, and rum together in a double boiler. Whisk until smooth and set aside to cool.

Combine the egg yolks and ½ cup of the sugar in the bowl of a KitchenAid stand mixer fitted with the whisk attachment and whip on high speed until thick, about 3 minutes. Reduce the speed to medium-low and pour in the chocolate mixture until blended. Slowly add in the flour and the salt and mix until blended.

Wash and dry the whisk attachment. Put the egg whites in a clean mixer bowl, fit the mixer with the clean whisk, and beat on medium speed until frothy. Increase the speed to high and whip until soft peaks form. Slowly add the remaining ⅓ cup sugar and whip until stiff peaks form.

Using a spatula, fold half of the egg whites into the chocolate batter. When almost completely incorporated, fold in the remaining egg whites just until no white streaks remain. Gently spread the batter into the prepared pan.

Bake until a skewer inserted into the center comes out clean, about 35 minutes. Let cool to room temperature. Line a baking sheet with parchment paper. Run a knife around the inside edge of the cake pan to loosen the cake, invert a wire rack on top of the cake and invert the pan and rack together. Lift off the pan. Place the rack on the prepared baking sheet.

TO MAKE THE CHOCOLATE GLAZE: In a small, heavy saucepan, bring the cream to a boil over high heat. Remove from the heat, add the chocolate, and whisk until smooth. Let the glaze cool until it thickens slightly but is still pourable, 30 to 60 minutes.

Slowly pour the glaze evenly over the top of the cake, allowing it to run down the sides. When the glaze stops dripping, use a large metal spatula to transfer the cake to a serving platter. Let the glaze continue to set before serving, about 1 hour. Cut the cake with a hot, dry knife. Serve with chantilly cream (recipe follows).

Chantilly Cream

MAKES 2 CUPS

1 cup heavy whipping cream

3 tablespoons sugar

½ teaspoon vanilla extract

In the bowl of a KitchenAid stand mixer fitted with the whisk attachment, whisk the cream, sugar, and vanilla until soft peaks form. Refrigerate until ready to use.

Molten Chocolate Cake

SERVES 10 *This is not so much a cake,
as a luscious, liquid centered soufflé.
Save this for impressing friends (or one special loved one) or
for when you don't mind being in the kitchen for the last minute
preparations. The recipe may be halved for those smaller, more
intimate gatherings.*

Truffle Centers

6 ounces bittersweet Couverture Chocolate,
  finely chopped

½ cup plus 1 tablespoon whipping Cream

Soufflé

½ pound (2 sticks) unsalted butter,
  cut into large pieces

10 ounces bittersweet Couverture Chocolate,
  finely chopped

4 large eggs

4 large egg yolks

½ cup sugar

2 tablespoons all-purpose flour

1 teaspoon instant espresso

TO MAKE THE TRUFFLE CENTERS: Place the chopped
chocolate in a heat-proof bowl. Bring the cream to a scald
in a small saucepan over medium-high heat and immediately pour over the chocolate. Let sit for a few minutes,
and then whisk until smooth. Cool to room temperature,
cover, and freeze until firm, at least 6 hours or overnight.

Scoop out balls of the chocolate mixture with a teaspoon
to make 10 small, marble-shaped truffles. Flatten them
into fat discs. Store in the freezer until needed. These can
be made a month ahead and stored in an airtight container in the freezer.

TO MAKE THE SOUFFLÉ: Preheat oven to 425°F. Butter and
flour ten ½ cup ceramic ramekins very thoroughly. There
should be no bare spots.

Melt the butter and chocolate together in a double boiler
or microwave. Whisk to combine until smooth. Set aside.

In the bowl of a KitchenAid stand mixer, whip the eggs,
egg yolks, and the sugar together on high speed, using
whisk attachment, until light and fluffy, about 2 minutes.

Fold the chocolate into the egg mixture. Sift the flour and
espresso over the bowl and fold in gently.

Spoon the batter into the ramekins to fill halfway. Nestle
a truffle in the center and fill the ramekin with the
remaining soufflé mixture. (They can be refrigerated at
this point for up to 6 hours. Bring to room temperature
before proceeding).

Bake for 8 to 9 minutes. The edges will be dry and come
away from the sides of the ramekins, but the center will
be soft. Remove from the oven and let sit two minutes.

Carefully loosen the edges of each cake and quickly invert
the ramekins onto individual plates. Serve immediately
with a scoop of vanilla ice cream.

Double Chocolate Ice Cream Sandwiches

By Emily Luchetti. Reprinted with permission from *A Passion for Ice Cream* (Chronicle Books 2006).

MAKES 10 SANDWICHES *Rich, home-made chocolate ice cream is sandwiched between fudge-like cookies for an unforgettable treat.*

Chocolate–Chocolate Chunk Ice Cream

6 large egg yolks

¾ cup sugar

⅛ teaspoon kosher salt

2 cups whole milk

2 cups heavy whipping cream

⅓ cup unsweetened cocoa powder

4 ounces bittersweet chocolate, chopped

Fudge Cookies

2 ounces (4 tablespoons) unsalted butter

12 ounces bittersweet chocolate, coarsely chopped

½ cup all-purpose flour

¼ teaspoon baking powder

Kosher salt

3 large eggs

¾ cup sugar

1 teaspoon vanilla extract

TO MAKE THE CHOCOLATE–CHOCOLATE CHUNK ICE CREAM: In a bowl, whisk together the egg yolks, ¼ cup of the sugar, and the salt in a bowl. Combine the milk, cream, and the remaining ½ cup sugar in a heavy saucepan. Cook over medium heat, stirring occasionally, until almost simmering. Slowly whisk the milk and cream into the egg mixture. Whisk in the cocoa powder. Return the cocoa mixture to the saucepan. Cook over medium-low heat, stirring constantly with a heat-resistant plastic or wooden spatula, until the custard reaches 175°F and lightly coats the spatula.

Strain the custard into a clean bowl and cool over an ice bath until room temperature. Refrigerate the custard for at least 4 hours or up to overnight. Put the chopped chocolate in a bowl and put the bowl in the freezer. Churn the ice cream using the ice cream attachment attached to a KitchenAid stand mixer. Fold the ice cream into the coarsely chopped chocolate. Freeze until it is hard enough to scoop, about 4 hours, depending on your freezer.

TO MAKE THE FUDGE COOKIES: Preheat the oven to 350°F. Line 3 baking sheets with parchment paper. Melt the butter and chocolate together in a double boiler over hot water. Stir to combine. Let cool to room temperature.

Sift together the flour and baking powder. Add the salt. In the bowl of a KitchenAid stand mixer using the whisk attachment, whip the eggs, sugar, and vanilla extract together on high speed until thick. By hand, stir in the cooled chocolate mixture. Stir in the flour mixture and let the batter sit for 5 minutes.

Using an ice cream scoop, using about 2 tablespoons (about 1¾ inches in diameter) for each cookie, scoop the batter onto the prepared pans and place at least 2 inches apart. There should be 20 cookies. Bake for about 10 minutes, or until the tops crack. They will look set and no longer shiny on top. Let cool and then remove them from the pans with a spatula.

Place 10 of the cookies, bottom side up, on a baking sheet lined with parchment or waxed paper. Place a scoop of ice cream on top of each cookie. Top with a second cookie and gently press down on the top cookie to adhere the sandwiches together. Serve immediately, or freeze until ready to serve.

Chocolate Caramel Pecan Squares

MAKES 115 SQUARES *These are just the kind of delicious, chewy chocolate nut morsels that everyone looks forward to eating over the holidays.*

Crust

1⅔ cups flour

¼ teaspoon baking powder

¼ teaspoon kosher salt

16 tablespoons (2 sticks) unsalted butter, softened

½ cup brown sugar

1 teaspoon vanilla extract

Filling

4 large eggs

½ cup sugar

¾ cup light corn syrup

6 tablespoons unsalted butter, melted

¼ teaspoon salt

1¼ cups pecans, toasted

1 cup mini chocolate chips

Preheat the oven to 350°F.

Grease the bottom and sides of a 9-by-13-inch pan. Line with a double layer of parchment paper, greasing between each layer of parchment, and again on top.

TO MAKE THE CRUST: Sift together the flour, baking powder, and salt.

In a KitchenAid stand mixer, cream the butter on medium speed until smooth. Add the brown sugar and vanilla extract and beat for 2 more minutes. Add the sifted dry ingredients on low speed and mix until just combined. Press the dough evenly into bottom of the pan.

Prick the dough with a fork every few inches. Bake about 20 minutes until golden brown.

TO MAKE THE FILLING: The filling needs to be ready to pour into the crust immediately after it comes out of the oven.

In a medium bowl, whisk the eggs and sugar. Whisk in the light corn syrup and the melted butter and salt. Stir in the pecans and chocolate chips. Pour the filling over the hot crust.

Bake until golden brown and set, about 25 minutes.

Cool completely on a wire rack before cutting. To cut, run a knife around the inside edge of the pan. Place a cookie sheet on top of the pan. Invert the pan and cookie sheet. Remove the pan and carefully peel off the parchment paper. Place a cutting board on top of the crust and invert the cookie sheet and the cutting board, turning the bars right side up. Cut the bars into 1-inch squares.

Karen's Chocolate Peppermint Bourbon Walnut Fudge

By Marcel Desaulniers. Reprinted with permission from
I'm Dreaming of a Chocolate Christmas, published by John
Wiley & Sons (2007).

MAKES ABOUT 3 POUNDS *This heavenly fudge recipe,
which is easy and nearly foolproof, comes from chocolate master
Marcel Desaulniers, prolific cookbook author and chef/owner
of the renowned Trellis Restaurant in Williamsburg, Virginia.*

3⅓ cups granulated sugar

1⅓ cups heavy cream

2 ounces (½ stick) unsalted butter, cut into 4 pieces

1 teaspoon salt

16 ounces semisweet baking chocolate,
   coarsely chopped

1 cup walnuts, toasted and coarsely chopped

1 tablespoon bourbon

1 tablespoon peppermint extract

Lightly coat the insides of an 8-by-8-by-2-inch nonstick
baking pan with 1 tablespoon melted butter (or spray with
vegetable oil spray), then line the pan with plastic wrap.
Set aside.

Heat the sugar, heavy cream, butter, and salt in a medium
sauce pan over medium heat. Bring to a boil, stirring frequently to completely dissolve the sugar. Turn the heat
down (so the mixture does not boil out of the saucepan),
and continue to boil while stirring frequently until the
mixture reaches a temperature of 230°F, about 6 minutes.

Remove from the heat. Add the chopped chocolate to
the very hot mixture and stir carefully (to avoid a pain-
ful burn) with a whisk until the chocolate has melted and
is completely incorporated. Add the walnuts, bourbon,
and peppermint extract and stir with a rubber spatula

until incorporated. Pour the fudge into the prepared pan,
spreading it evenly with the rubber spatula. Cover with
plastic wrap, then refrigerate until firm, about 2 hours.

TO SERVE: Remove the top layer of plastic wrap. Flip the
pan upside down on top of a cutting board. Remove the
plastic wrap. Cut into desired size pieces. Store in a tightly
sealed plastic container in the refrigerator. Bring to room
temperature before serving.

Chocolate Amaretto Terrine

By Marcel Desaulniers. Reprinted with permission from *I'm Dreaming of a Chocolate Christmas*, published by John Wiley & Sons (2007)

SERVES 10 TO 12 *The secret flavors in this dense chocolate and surprisingly easy dessert are almonds and amaretto. It can be made several weeks ahead and kept tightly wrapped in the freezer. Serve with a dollop of unsweetened whipped cream.*

- 24 ounces semisweet baking chocolate, coarsely chopped
- 3⅓ cups heavy cream
- 2 cups sliced almonds, toasted and coarsely chopped
- 2 ounces amaretto

Lightly spray the insides of a 9-by-5-by-2½-inch terrine pan with vegetable oil spray, then line the pan with plastic wrap. Set aside.

Place the semisweet chocolate in a large bowl.

Heat the heavy cream in a medium sauce pan over medium-high heat. Bring to a boil, then remove from the heat. Pour the boiling cream over the chocolate and stir with a whisk until smooth.

Add the toasted almonds and the amaretto, using a rubber spatula to fold them into the chocolate mixture. Pour the chocolate mixture into the terrine pan. Cover the top of the terrine with plastic wrap, then place in the freezer overnight.

TO SERVE: Remove the terrine from the pan (if it does not slide out, use a cake spatula or similar thin bladed spatula and pass the spatula around the inside edges between the plastic wrap and the pan), then remove and discard the plastic wrap. Heat the blade of a serrated slicer under hot running water and wipe the blade dry before cutting each slice. This slim terrine weighs in at a hefty 60 ounces, so you should be able to cut ten to twelve 5- to 5¾-ounce slices.

Bittersweet Chocolate Fondue

By Emily Luchetti. Reprinted with permission from *A Passion for Desserts* (Chronicle Books, 2003).

MAKES 8 SERVINGS *You do not need a fondue pot to make this simple, but delicious chocolate treat. Just put out lots of "dippers" and you have an instant celebration.*

- ½ cup heavy whipping cream
- ½ cup milk
- 11 ounces bittersweet chocolate, finely chopped

Warm the cream and milk in a medium saucepan over medium heat until hot and bubbling around the edges, about 5 minutes. Remove from the heat. Add the chopped chocolate, let sit for 30 seconds, and then whisk until smooth. Pour the chocolate into small decorative bowls.

Place the bowls on the table along with a platter of items to be dipped. Serve with long forks to make dipping easier.

SUGGESTIONS FOR "DIPPERS"
(ALLOW AT LEAST 6 ITEMS PER PERSON)

- Small ice cream balls coated in cookie crumbs
- Marshmallows
- Biscotti
- Graham crackers
- Banana chunks
- Almonds
- Caramels
- Mini profiteroles
- Angel food cake cubes
- Pound cake cubes
- Pretzels
- Mini coconut macaroons

Holiday Gifts
from the Kitchen

Spiced Mixed Olives

MAKES 4 CUPS *Olives have come into their own in the last few years and make a wonderful snack or appetizer for guests. Pack these into a mason jar and you have an eye-catching holiday gift which your recipients will appreciate as a healthy alternative to holiday sweets.*

½ pound large green olives

½ pound large Kalamata olives

Zest of 1 lemon, roughly chopped

2 teaspoons dried oregano, crumbled

½ teaspoon red pepper flakes

2 teaspoon fennel seeds

2 large bay leaves

½ teaspoons ground black pepper

1¼ cups olive oil, plus more as needed

Pat the olives dry with paper towels and lightly crush them with your hand, just to break the skin. Place in a container with a tight fitting lid.

In a heavy saucepan, combine the lemon zest, oregano, pepper flakes, fennel, bay leaves, black pepper, and olive oil. Bring just barely to a simmer.

Pour over the olives to cover the olives completely. Let stand, uncovered, at room temperature for 4 hours. Cover and refrigerate for at least 2 days to allow the flavors to blend. Can be stored in the refrigerator for up to 2 months.

Serve at room temperature.

Spiced Nuts

MAKES 2⅓ CUPS *The exotic and alluring aroma of the cumin, the kick of the cayenne and the extra dose of sweetness make these nuts irresistible. They will keep their flavor in an air-tight jar for weeks.*

2 tablespoons vegetable oil

1½ teaspoons cumin

¼ teaspoon cayenne pepper

2 tablespoons sugar

1 teaspoon salt

2½ cups mixed nuts of your choice

Preheat oven to 300°F.

Heat the oil in a heavy saucepan over medium-low heat. Add the cumin and cayenne and stir until the mix becomes aromatic, about 15 seconds.

Pour the flavored oil over the nuts. Add the sugar and salt and mix to coat well. Transfer the nuts to a baking pan and bake, stirring occasionally for about 20 minutes. Let cool and transfer to a bowl to serve.

Sweet Cinnamon Pecans

By Emily Luchetti. Reprinted with permission from *Classic Stars Desserts* (Chronicle Books 2007).

MAKES 4½ CUPS *Easy to make, these cinnamon-flavored pecans end up with a crunchy, sweet crust. They make a great gift or toss a few onto a dish of ice cream along with some chocolate shavings for a quick, but elegant holiday dessert.*

1 large egg white
2 teaspoons vanilla extract
½ cup firmly packed light brown sugar
2 tablespoons ground cinnamon
4⅓ cups (14 to 16 ounces) pecan halves

Preheat the oven to 300°F.

In a bowl, whisk together the egg white and vanilla until frothy. Stir in the brown sugar, cinnamon, and pecans until the nuts are evenly coated. Spread the pecans evenly on a baking sheet.

Toast, stirring every 10 minutes, until the nuts are dry, about 30 minutes. Remove from the oven and let cool to room temperature. Transfer to a bowl and serve.

Crispy Almond Cheese Balls

MAKES 18 PIECES *After trying just one, someone called these "love at first bite." A crunchy, nutty coating encases a warm, creamy cheese filling. For best results, be sure to get high quality cheeses.*

½ cup coarsely chopped blanched almonds
⅓ cup Panko crumbs or crushed cornflakes
1 cup shredded Swiss cheese
1 cup shredded aged Cheddar cheese
¼ cup all-purpose flour
¼ teaspoon cayenne pepper
¼ teaspoon ground white pepper
Salt
2 large egg whites
½ cup vegetable oil

Combine the almonds and panko crumbs in a small bowl and set aside.

In another bowl, mix together the Swiss cheese, Cheddar cheese, flour, cayenne, white pepper, and a pinch of salt.

Using a KitchenAid stand mixer, whip the egg whites until they are stiff. Fold the whipped whites into the cheese mixture.

Scoop 1 tablespoon of the cheese mixture and form into a ball. Roll in the almond-panko mixture and place on a cookie sheet. Repeat with the remaining cheese mixture. Refrigerate for at least 1 hour or up to 24 hours.

In a skillet, heat the oil. Cook the cheese balls in small batches until golden brown, turning often, 2 to 3 minutes. Transfer to paper towels to drain. Serve warm.

The cheese balls can be cooled and reheated in a 400°F. oven for 8 to 10 minutes until heated through.

Black Bean Soup Mix

Because they have a long shelf life, you can make these inexpensive gift jars months ahead of the holidays. There are a number of ways to personalize these jars with decorations. Choose fabrics or lace to place over the lid, then tie with a ribbon that holds the recipe card.

1½ cups black beans

1 teaspoon cumin

1 teaspoon chili powder

½ teaspoon garlic powder

½ teaspoon black pepper

1 tablespoon dried minced onion

2 chicken bouillon cubes

1½ cups uncooked pasta shells, medium

Put the black beans into a 1 quart food storage jar with an air-tight lid. Mix together all the spices and place into a small, sealable food storage bag. Place on top of the beans and smooth out so the bag is laying flat. Pour the pasta into the jar and seal.

Black Bean Soup Recipe

SERVES 8

1 jar Black Bean Soup Mix

6 cups water

1 cup diced tomatoes with liquid

Ham bone (optional)

1 cup carrots, diced small (optional)

1 cup zucchini, diced small (optional)

Cover the beans with 2 inches of water and let soak overnight.

In a soup pot, add the soaked beans, 6 cups of water, tomatoes, seasonings from the soup mix, and ham bone if using. Bring to a boil over high heat, then reduce heat to low, cover the soup and allow to simmer for approximately 2 hours until the beans are tender. Add the pasta, carrots, and zucchini and continue cooking for 10 minutes until tender. Remove the ham bone. Taste and adjust the seasoning for salt and pepper. Serve.

Cookies in a Jar

Excerpted from *A Baker's Field Guide to Cupcakes*, by Dede Wilson. © 2006, used by permission from The Harvard Common Press.

"Cookies in a jar" is a creative, inexpensive gift-giving idea that has become very popular. The first part of the recipe contains instructions for layering the dry cookie ingredients in a jar to give as a gift, while the second part is the recipe you want to print out on a card and attach to the jar with a pretty ribbon. Success in preparing the jars lies in making the layers of ingredients even and packing each one down as you go.

1¾ cups all-purpose flour

1 teaspoon baking soda

¼ teaspoon salt

¾ up light brown sugar, firmly packed

½ cup sugar

¼ cup Dutch-processed unsweetened cocoa powder, sifted

½ cup finely chopped walnuts

½ cup semisweet chocolate chips

½ cup candy coated chocolates, such as M&M's

1 quart decorative jar with lid

Whisk the flour, baking soda, and salt together in a bowl.

Make sure the decorative jar is clean, sterile, and dry. Pour the flour mixture into the jar and pack down firmly into an even layer. Pour the brown sugar into the jar and tamp down to form an even layer. Follow with an even layer of the sugar, and another of the cocoa powder. You may need to wipe the sides of the jar down after the cocoa as some of it may cling. Add a layer of nuts, a layer of the chocolate chips, and a layer of the candies and tamp them down.

Screw the top on the jar and seal tightly.

Add a decorative note card and any decorations you wish to the outside of the jar.

Cookies in a Jar Recipe

MAKES 30 COOKIES

1½ sticks butter (melted and cooled)

1 large egg

1 teaspoon vanilla extract

Contents of Cookies in a Jar

Preheat oven to 350°F and line two baking sheets with parchment paper.

Put the cooled, melted butter in a large bowl, whisk in the egg and vanilla extract. Add the contents of the jar and stir until well combined; you might need to use your hands. Drop by generously rounded tablespoon, 2 inches apart, on prepared cookie sheets and press to flatten.

Bake until tops are cracked and dry; they will be soft on top and in the middle, about 12 minutes.

Cookies will firm up during cooling. Slide parchment paper onto cooling racks and cool completely.

Cookies can be stored at room temperature in a sealed container for up to a week.

Walnut Caramels with Sea Salt

MAKES ABOUT SIXTY 1-INCH CARAMELS *These delicious caramels are enhanced by the flavors of toasted walnuts and sea salt. They make an attractive presentation when wrapped in parchment paper. Simply cut parchment rectangles approximately one inch longer than the caramels, wrap the candy in the center, and twist the ends.*

- 2 cups cream
- ⅔ cup light corn syrup
- ⅔ cup honey
- 1 cup sugar
- 4 ounces softened unsalted butter
- ½ teaspoon kosher salt
- ½ teaspoon pure vanilla extract
- 8 ounces walnuts, toasted and chopped
- ¼ teaspoon sea salt

Grease the bottom and sides of a 9-by-9-inch baking dish. Line the bottom with parchment paper. Grease the top of the parchment paper.

Combine the cream, corn syrup, honey and sugar in a large pot. Cook over medium heat, stirring often, to 260°F, about 15 minutes.

Remove from the heat. Stir in the butter, kosher salt, and vanilla. Fold in the walnuts and pour into the baking dish. Sprinkle the sea salt over the caramels and let cool.

Run a knife around the inside edge of the pan and invert on to a cutting board. Cut into 1-inch pieces and roll individually in waxed paper.

Double Chocolate Peppermint Bark

Excerpted from *A Baker's Field Guide to Holiday Candy and Confections,* by Dede Wilson. © 2003, used by permission from The Harvard Common Press.

MAKES ABOUT 2 POUNDS *This crunchy, minty confection is great for gift giving.*

- Twelve 6- or 7-inch peppermint candy canes
- 1 pound bittersweet or semisweet couverture chocolate, finely chopped
- 1 pound white couverture chocolate, finely chopped

Line a jelly-roll pan with aluminum foil, shiny side up, smoothing out any wrinkles.

Place the candy canes in a heavy-duty Ziploc plastic bag and seal the bag. Using a rolling pin, crush the candy canes until they are fairly uniformly crushed. Aim for ¼-inch pieces. If there is a lot of powdery residue, place the candy in a strainer and shake out the powdery part (you can save it and stir it into hot chocolate). Set the crushed candy aside. You may also chop the candy canes in a KitchenAid food processor fitted with a metal blade, pulsing on and off. It will make a racket, however.

Temper the bittersweet chocolate and using an offset spatula, spread in an even, thin layer (about ⅛-inch thin) all over the aluminum foil. It doesn't have to be perfectly rectangular. The candy will be broken up into pieces. Refrigerate the chocolate while you temper white chocolate.

Take the tempered white chocolate and spread in an even, thin layer over the refrigerated bittersweet chocolate. Immediately sprinkle chopped peppermint candy over the white chocolate while it is still wet. Refrigerate until completely firm, about 20 minutes. Break the bark into irregular pieces and enjoy!

Cacao Bean Bittersweet Chocolate Truffles

Excerpted from *Truffles*, by Dede Wilson.
© 2006, used by permission from The Harvard Common Press.

MAKES 55 PIECES *Cacao beans, from which we get all of our wonderful chocolate, are now available to the consumer in a raw form. Cacao nibs are not sweet but they have an intense chocolate flavor unlike any other product. In this recipe they are steeped in the cream to add flavor, are found in the ganache to add texture (you will need Sharffen Berger Nibby Bars) and are chopped and used as a topping.*

- 1 cup heavy whipping cream
- ¼ cup plus 4 teaspoons cacao nibs
- 10 ounces Scharffen Berger Nibby Bar Chocolate, 8 ounces finely chopped and 2 ounces in rough chunks
- Dutch-processed cocoa
- 55 small fluted paper cups (optional)

Pour the cream into a 2-quart, wide saucepan. Add ¼ cup of the cacao nibs to the cream and heat over medium heat until it barely comes to a simmer. Remove from heat and let sit for 10 minutes. Strain out the nibs and discard. Return the pan to the heat and bring to a simmer. Remove from the heat and immediately sprinkle the 8 ounces finely chopped chocolate into the cream. Cover and let it sit for 5 minutes-the heat should melt the chocolate. Stir very gently (you don't want to incorporate air) until smooth.

If the chocolate isn't melting, place the saucepan over very low heat and stir until smooth, but take care not to let it get too hot or it will burn.

Pour the mixture—now called a ganache—into a shallow bowl and cover with plastic wrap. Let it cool at room temperature, preferably overnight, or until firm enough to roll. (You may refrigerate the ganache until it is firm enough to roll, about 4 hours).

Place the remaining chocolate and nibs in the bowl of a KitchenAid food processor fitted with a metal blade. Pulse on and off until both are finely ground but not powdery (they should retain some texture). Place in a small bowl. Coat your hands with cocoa and roll the ganache into ¾- to 1-inch balls. These should be as round as possible, but they don't need to be perfect.

Toss each truffle in the chocolate-cacao nib coating. Place in fluted paper cups (if using) and serve at room temperature.

Caramel Sauce

By Emily Luchetti. Reprinted with permission from *Classic Stars Desserts* (Chronicle Books, 2007).

MAKES 1¾ CUPS *This recipe, which originally came from James Beard, makes a wonderful hostess gift. Spoon it warm over ice cream for a quick dessert. This sauce can be made up to 2 weeks in advance, covered and refrigerated.*

- 1½ cups sugar
- ½ cup water
- 1 cup heavy whipping cream
- 1½ ounces (3 tablespoons) unsalted butter

Stir together the sugar and the water in a medium saucepan and cook over medium heat until the sugar is dissolved, about 5 minutes. Brush the insides of the pan with a pastry brush dipped in water to eliminate any sugar sticking to the sides. Increase the heat to high and cook without stirring until the sugar is amber colored, 8 to 10 minutes. Remove the pot from the heat.

Wearing oven mitts, slowly add one quarter cup of the cream. Be careful as the caramel will sputter as the cream is added. Using a wooden spoon or heat resistant spatula, stir the cream into the caramel. If the cream sputters, stop stirring. Let the bubbles subside and then stir again.

Carefully add the remaining cream and stir until combined. Whisk in the butter. Pour into decorative jars and tie with a pretty ribbon.

Cappuccino Fudge Sauce

MAKES 1½ CUPS *With coffee and brandy accents, this is a luxurious fudge sauce that comes together in minutes. It can be stored in the refrigerator for up to 2 weeks.*

- 1¼ cups whipping cream, or as needed
- 2 tablespoon instant espresso
- ¼ cup sugar
- 6 ounces semisweet chocolate, finely chopped
- 2 tablespoon brandy

Combine the cream, sugar, and espresso in a heavy saucepan over high heat. Bring to a boil and remove from the heat. Add the chocolate and stir until melted. Add the brandy.

Pour into sterilized mason jars and seal tightly. Tie with a festive ribbon.

Limoncello

Limoncello, a sweet lemon liqueur, whose origins are from Southern Italy, is inexpensive to make and a real treat. Remember that it takes 80 days to make, so you have to start planning early if you want to give it as a gift.

12 lemons
2 bottles (750ml each) 100 proof vodka
4½ cups sugar
5 cups water

Wash the lemons well in warm water. Zest the lemons and place into a 4-quart mason jar. Pour in one of the bottles of vodka, stir, and store in a dark closet at room temperature for 40 days.

On the 40th day, make a syrup by stirring the sugar and water together and bringing to a boil in a large sauce pan. Boil for about 5 minutes, remove from the heat, and cool. Add the syrup to the mason jar along with the second bottle of vodka. Place back into the dark closet for another 40 days. Use a coffee filter or several layers of cheesecloth to strain the limoncello into smaller bottles which can be stored in the freezer until ready for giving.

New Year's Day Brunch

Broiled Grapefruit with Vanilla-Ginger Sugar

SERVES 6 *Crystallized ginger—ginger root which has been dried and preserved with sugar--has a wonderful spicy-sweet flavor that's a perfect match with broiled grapefruit. It should be readily available in many supermarkets, especially around winter holidays.*

⅔ cup sugar

3 tablespoons chopped crystallized ginger

¾ teaspoon pure vanilla extract

6 large pink grapefruit

Preheat the broiler.

In the bowl of a KitchenAid food processor, pulse the sugar, ginger and vanilla until finely ground.

Halve each grapefruit crosswise and run a knife around each section to loosen the membrane. Arrange the grapefruits, cut side up, in a baking dish just large enough to hold them in one layer. Sprinkle the tops with the sugar mixture.

Broil the grapefruit about 1½ inches from the heat until the sugar melts and the tops begin to brown, about 10 to 15 minutes.

Serve at room temperature.

Brown Sugar Bacon with Mustard

SERVES 6 *A simple topping of brown sugar and mustard turns ordinary bacon into a special treat for brunch.*

1 pound thick-cut bacon

2 tablespoons light brown sugar, lightly packed

1 tablespoon Dijon mustard

Black pepper

The night before, cook the bacon in a pan over medium-high heat until three-quarters of the way done, about 3 minutes on each side The bacon should be just starting to brown and have released most of its fat. Drain the bacon on paper towels.

While the bacon is cooking, combine the brown sugar and mustard in a small bowl to make a paste.

Arrange the bacon in an even layer in a 13-by-9-inch baking dish. Spread the brown sugar paste over the bacon as evenly as possible. Season with a few grinds of black pepper. Cover with plastic wrap and refrigerate overnight.

The next day, preheat the oven to 350°F. Bake the bacon, uncovered, for 5 to 10 minutes, or until it's as crisp as you like it. Serve immediately.

Apple Cranberry Croissant Breakfast Pudding

SERVES 6 *Bread pudding goes upscale, using flaky croissant instead of plain bread. The classic sweet-tart flavors of apple and cranberry fit right into the holiday spirit and the light streusel topping gives it that extra festive touch. This can be assembled the day before and stored in the refrigerator until it needs to be baked.*

    4 croissants cut into 1-inch cubes (about 5½ cups)

    2 apples, such as Cortland or Granny Smith,
        peeled, cored, and diced

    1 cup dried cranberries

    2 cups whole milk

    1 cup whipping cream

    ⅔ cup sugar

    4 large eggs

    1 teaspoon vanilla extract

    ½ teaspoon cinnamon

    ½ cup chopped walnuts

    ½ cup light brown sugar, lightly packed

    2 tablespoons (¼ stick) unsalted butter, melted

    ¼ cup all-purpose flour

Spray a 9-by-13-inch pan with oil or other cooking spray.

Spread the cubed croissants evenly over the bottom of the baking dish. Scatter the apples and cranberries over the croissants and toss together lightly, spreading the mixture evenly throughout the pan.

In the bowl of a KitchenAid stand mixer, beat on medium speed the milk, cream, and sugar until the sugar begins to dissolve. Add in the eggs, one at a time, then the vanilla and the cinnamon. Pour the mixture over the croissant mixture in the pan. Press the croissants down to absorb the liquid and let sit at least 30 minutes, or cover with plastic wrap and refrigerate overnight. Be sure to remove the mixture from the refrigerator before preheating the oven in the morning.

Preheat the oven to 350°F.

Combine the walnuts, brown sugar, melted butter, and flour in a small bowl. Sprinkle evenly over the bread pudding mixture. Bake for about 40 minutes or until puffed and lightly golden. The custard should be set.

Let cool on a wire rack for 10 minutes. Serve warm or at room temperature.

Herbed Salmon Cakes with Cilantro-Caper Mayonnaise

SERVES 4 *If you're a fan of crab cakes, here is a delightful salmon variation that is equally delicious and economical. The tarragon and lemon flavors add great flavor, as do the cilantro and capers in the mayonnaise. These tasty little cakes are very versatile—serve them for brunch, as a first course, or as the main course paired with a steamy bowl of soup and a green leafy salad.*

Cilantro-Caper Mayonnaise

3 tablespoons lightly packed fresh cilantro leaves

½ cup mayonnaise or salad dressing

1 tablespoon drained capers

Salmon Cakes

2 cups French or Italian bread cubes

1 tablespoon fresh tarragon leaves

1 strip lemon peel, yellow portion only

2 green onions, cut into 1-inch pieces

½ rib celery, cut into 1-inch pieces

1 egg

2 teaspoons lemon juice

¼ teaspoon salt

⅛ teaspoon black pepper

1 pound fresh salmon fillets, grilled or
   broiled, and skin removed, or
   two 7-ounce cans salmon, drained

1 tablespoon olive oil

1 tablespoon butter

TO MAKE THE CILANTRO-CAPER MAYONNAISE: Position a mini bowl and mini blade in the work bowl of a KitchenAid food processor. With the motor running, add the cilantro. Process 8 to 10 seconds until chopped. Scrape the sides of bowl and add the mayonnaise and the capers. Process 10 to 12 seconds until completely mixed. Transfer to a small bowl, cover and refrigerate.

TO MAKE THE SALMON CAKES: Using the multipurpose blade in the work bowl of the food processor, process the bread cubes until fine crumbs form, about 20 seconds. Transfer the crumbs to a shallow pan. With the motor running, add the tarragon, lemon peel, and onions and process 5 to 8 seconds until chopped. Scrape the sides of the bowl. Add the celery and pulse 2 to 3 times until chopped. Add the egg, lemon juice, salt, pepper, and ¾ cup of the bread crumbs. Pulse 2 to 3 times more until mixed. Add the salmon and pulse 5 to 6 times just until mixed. The mixture will be soft. Chill, if desired, for easier handling.

Shape the mixture into 4 cakes, about ½-inch thick. Coat both sides of cakes with the remaining bread crumbs and set aside on a plate.

In a large skillet over medium heat, warm the oil and butter. Add the salmon cakes and cook 5 to 8 minutes, or until golden brown and heated through, turning once. Serve with Cilantro-Caper Mayonnaise.

Spinach and Goat Cheese Breakfast Frittata

SERVES 8 *While a French omelet is cooked quickly over high heat, Italian frittatas are cooked more slowly, allowing you to relax with your guests while your oven does the work. This version has an abundance of cheese which when combined with eggs and spinach, offer up some delicious results.*

9 large eggs

2 cups cottage cheese

5 ounces shredded cheddar cheese (about 1⅔ cup)

5 ounces soft goat cheese, such as Montrachet, crumbled

½ teaspoon salt

½ teaspoon pepper

10 ounce package frozen chopped spinach, thawed

½ pint cherry or grape tomatoes, quartered

Preheat the oven to 350°F. Spray a 9-by-13-inch baking dish with oil or other cooking spray.

In a large bowl, whisk the eggs until they're frothy. Whisk in the cottage cheese, cheddar, goat cheese, salt, and pepper.

Put the thawed spinach in a colander and press any excess water out with the back of a large spoon. Add the drained spinach and tomato pieces to the egg mixture and combine well. Pour the mixture into the prepared baking dish.

Bake for about 35 minutes or until the eggs are set. The frittata will be puffed and golden around the edges.

Scotch Eggs

SERVES 6 *Emily Luchetti first tried this unique brunch dish— hard boiled eggs wrapped in sausage, breaded, and then pan fried—at a party in San Francisco where they flew off the serving tray. Despite their name, scotch eggs originated in England and are a traditional picnic food served at room temperature.*

1 pound bulk spicy sausage

1 teaspoon chopped fresh thyme

1 teaspoon chopped fresh rosemary

⅓ cup bread crumbs

1 egg, lightly beaten

6 hard boiled eggs

Vegetable or corn oil

Mustard (optional)

Mix together the sausage, thyme and rosemary. Divide the meat into 6 portions.

Sprinkle a few bread crumbs on a work surface. Pat the sausage meat into a 2½ inch circle. Wrap it around a hard boiled egg, completely covering it. Make sure the egg is not showing. Roll the egg in bread crumbs and dip in the beaten egg. Repeat with the remaining eggs.

In a large heavy duty frying pan, add the vegetable oil to a depth of about 1 inch. Heat the oil over a high heat and add the sausage-eggs. Fry until the sausage is thoroughly cooked and browned. Cool slightly before serving.

Cut in half or quarters to serve. If desired, serve with mustard.

Cornmeal Waffles with Goat Cheese and Sun-Dried Tomatoes

SERVES 5 TO 6 *Welcome in the New Year (or any day of the week) with this upscale version of waffles that is as easy to make as they are to eat. The citrus-flavored compound butter adds tremendous flavor to the waffles and is a refreshing alternative to heavy syrups.*

1¾ cups milk

8 ounces goat cheese

2 ounces sun-dried tomatoes

6 tablespoons melted butter

2 eggs, separated

1¼ cups all-purpose flour

¾ cup yellow cornmeal

2 tablespoons sugar

1 tablespoons baking powder

¾ teaspoon salt

Combine the milk, goat cheese, sun-dried tomatoes, melted butter and egg yolks in a KitchenAid blender and blend until incorporated. Add the flour, cornmeal, sugar, baking powder, and salt to the blender with the milk mixture and blend until smooth.

In the bowl of a KitchenAid stand mixer fitted with the wire whip, beat egg whites using the whisk attachment until soft peaks form. Fold the whipped whites into the batter.

Preheat a KitchenAid waffle iron. When hot, cook the waffles following the waffle iron instructions.

Serve with Lemon Thyme Compound Butter (recipe follows)

Lemon Thyme Compound Butter

2 sticks (8 ounces) butter, softened

1 lemon, zested and juiced

1 orange, zested and juiced

6 sprigs fresh thyme

1 teaspoon salt

Mix the butter, lemon zest and juice, orange zest and juice, thyme, and salt until well combined. Form into a roll, wrap in plastic, and refrigerate.

Chocolate Waffles

SERVES 8 *Chocolate waffles are a crowd pleaser that are as welcome at brunch as they are for dessert. Drizzle with chocolate or strawberry sauce if you like, but if you really want to gild the lily, add a dollop of whipped cream and a little fresh fruit or nuts.*

> 1 cup all-purpose flour
>
> ½ cup cocoa powder
>
> ¼ cup sugar
>
> 1 teaspoon baking powder
>
> ½ teaspoon baking soda
>
> ¼ teaspoon salt
>
> 2 large eggs at room temperature
>
> 1¼ cups milk at room temperature (12 ounces)
>
> 3 tablespoons butter, melted
>
> 1 teaspoon vanilla

Place the flour, cocoa powder, sugar, baking powder, baking soda, and salt into a bowl and using a whisk, mix thoroughly until well combined and there are no lumps.

Put the eggs, milk, and melted butter into a KitchenAid blender. Carefully add the sifted dry ingredients into the blender and mix together. Halfway through, stop the blender and scrape down the sides, then continue blending for another 30 seconds.

Pour about ½ cup of the batter into a greased, heated KitchenAid waffle iron. Cook 2 to 3 minutes until cooked through.

Stuffed French Toast

If you're nostalgic for the cream cheese and jelly sandwiches you ate as a kid, this recipe is for you. A decadently delicious brunch item, it has a sweet, cinnamon flavored crunchy coating and a creamy filling that oozes out with the first bite. For extra richness, use brioche bread.

> 8 slices high quality white bread
>
> 8 ounces whipped cream cheese
>
> 4 ounces fruit preserves (strawberry, blueberry, or raspberry)
>
> 3 eggs
>
> ½ cup heavy cream
>
> ½ teaspoon cinnamon
>
> ½ teaspoon vanilla
>
> 2 teaspoons sugar
>
> Salt
>
> 2 cups corn flakes, crushed
>
> 2 tablespoons butter

Spread 4 of the bread slices with cream cheese and the other 4 with preserves. Then make 4 sandwiches, each containing a slice of bread with cream cheese and preserves.

Using a KitchenAid handheld mixer, beat together the eggs, cream, cinnamon, vanilla, sugar, and a pinch of salt until well blended. Dip a sandwich in the egg batter to coat lightly on each side. Dip the sandwich in the crushed corn flakes to coat on both sides. Repeat with the other sandwiches.

Melt the butter in a skillet or griddle over medium heat and fry the sandwiches until they are golden brown on both sides. Add more butter as needed.

Home-Made Doughnuts

MAKES 24 DOUGHNUTS *People in Holland believe that eating doughnuts will bring good luck in the new year. That may or may not be true, but one thing is for sure--they will definitely bring fun into your kitchen, especially if you dip them in different toppings such as chocolate, nuts, or sprinkles.*

Doughnuts

1¼ cup milk

4 packages yeast

1 cup warm water (105°F)

¾ cup vegetable shortening

½ cup sugar

3 large eggs, beaten

2 teaspoon salt

8 cups all-purpose flour

2 cups vegetable oil

Glaze

⅔ cups boiling water

16 ounces powdered sugar

1 tablespoon vanilla extract

Optional toppings:

Melted chocolate (white and dark)

Sprinkles (chocolate or multi-colored)

Chocolate Jimmies

Mini chocolate chips

Chopped nuts

Crushed toffee

Shredded coconut

Cinnamon sugar

TO MAKE THE DOUGHNUTS: Heat the milk over high heat until almost boiling to scald. Set aside to cool to lukewarm. In a large mixing bowl stir together the yeast and the warm water (105°F.) and set aside for approximately 5 minutes until the yeast is foamy.

In the bowl of a KitchenAid stand mixer fitted with the paddle, add the shortening, sugar, eggs, and salt. Beat at medium speed to combine. Add the cooled milk and foamy yeast mixture and beat on medium until the ingredients are well mixed.

Switch to the dough hook and add the flour, 1 cup at a time, while mixing continuously at medium speed until the dough forms a ball that follows the hook around the bowl.

Transfer the dough to a lightly greased bowl and cover it lightly with a tea towel. Let rise for 30 minutes in a warm place.

Punch the dough down and transfer to a floured work surface. Roll the dough out to ½-inch thickness and, using a doughnut cutter, cut out the doughnuts. Cover them with a tea towel and let rise until double in bulk, about 45 minutes to an hour.

Heat the oil in a large skillet to 350°F. Fry the doughnuts in the oil, 3 to 4 at a time, turning as needed, until golden brown. Drain on paper towels.

TO MAKE THE GLAZE: In a medium bowl, mix the boiling water with the powdered sugar and beat well until smooth. Add the vanilla and stir until combined. Glaze the doughnuts while still warm.

OPTIONAL: dip the warm doughnuts in the toppings of your choice.

Index

Acknowledgments

Both *The Holiday Table* television series and the cookbook are the result of a collaboration between many tremendously talented people. First and foremost, we want to thank our hosts, Chris Fennimore, Emily Luchetti and Dede Wilson—three passionate and deeply knowledgeable culinary experts who contributed many of the recipes in this book and presented them on television with great charm and wit. They put their heart and soul into making sure the recipes and demonstrations would have great appeal to home cooks.

We were fortunate to have numerous guests who also contributed wonderful recipes to this cookbook including Tony Mantuano, chef at Chicago's famed *Spiagga* restaurant, Chef Jimmy Bannos of Chicago's *Heaven on Seven*, Joyce White, a leading author on soul cooking, and Mitchell Davis, renowned for his books on Jewish cooking.

In filming the shows, we brought in a number of tabletop experts, many of whom traveled long distances to share their culinary and tabletop knowledge. Isabelle von Boch from the legendary Villeroy & Boch china company, was a regular guest who—no matter what city we filmed in—always showed up dazzling us equally with her beautiful table settings, charm, and wealth of information. Macy's Susan Bertelsen not only lined up an amazing group of tabletop experts but designed and presented several beautiful holiday tables herself. Entertaining expert Maria McBride, author and editor of *Brides* magazine

was another regular whose creative holiday tables reflect her tremendous talents. We'd also like to thank the other design experts who appeared on the show including Lord Piers Wedgwood, Jim O'Leary, Jorge Perez, Carlo Mondavi, Paul Thompson, Edward Lent, Carolyne Roehm, Nancy Moussette, Durand Guion, and Harriette Cole. Another big thank you goes to Su Hilty from the wonderful merchandise mart, 7 W 34th in New York City. She has always been there for us with leads and advice when we had tabletop questions.

We'd also like to acknowledge our highly talented production staff whose hard work and creativity make our shows sparkle. Todd Gardiner, Michael Varga, Mike Tillotson, Colleen Corley, Phillip Messenger, Jonathan Dinerstein, John Heaman, Gloria Cabral, Matt Clarke, and Matthew Levie.

Of course, our biggest thanks and appreciation goes to KitchenAid and their staff who sponsored *The Holiday Table*, giving us both their financial and moral support at every step along the way. A big thank you to Brian Maynard, Deborah O'Connor, David Skinner, Marty Armstrong, Jeff McClure, Dave Svec, Bruce Roberson, and Tandy Ulleg.

And finally, a big thank you to the many hard-working and dedicated professionals in the PBS community who supported *The Holiday Table*.

—*Marjorie Poore*

90 Years –
Experience in Every Batch

Maybe you remember making cookies with your mom, or the smell of homemade bread wafting from the oven. Our stand mixers bring time-honored design and performance features to your kitchen. Rediscover what it's like to gather around the oven waiting for the first taste or share a home-cooked meal with your family.

Key Features

Choose a model with either a 4½- or 5-quart mixing bowl.

Standard accessories generally include: a flat beater for normal to heavy mixing, dough hook, and wire whip.

The beater spirals to 67 different touch-points within the bowl for quick, complete mixing.

Features a direct-drive transmission for reliable power delivery. Metal construction assures long-lasting, stable operation.

Get in the Mix

The tilt-head stand mixer gives you easy access to the beaters and bowl. Tilt the head back for access; tilt-down and lock for mixing. You can also mix it up in the kitchen with a wide array of colors.

Mix it up in the kitchen with a **wide array of colors.**

tilt-head stand mixers

You Put Your Heart into Every Bite They Take

You put the time and effort into making every dish. You'll bake a cake for any occasion, make cookies for all the neighborhood children, and look for reasons to bake your delectable homemade bread. KitchenAid has the stand mixer that will help you express your talents and creativity with the fresh ingredients and seasonings that truly make the meal your creation.

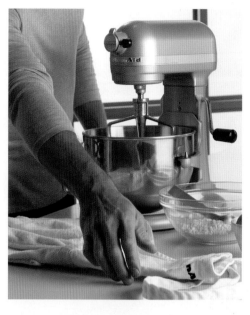

Key Features

Choose a model with either a 5- or 6-quart mixing bowl. Standard accessories include a dough hook, flat beater for general mixing, and a wire whip.

The beater spirals to 67 different touch-points within the bowl for quick, complete mixing.

The Soft Start® Mixing feature helps minimize ingredient splatter with gentle acceleration to the selected speed. The electronic speed sensor monitors operation to maintain the selected speed, regardless of the weight load.

Features an all-steel gear, direct-drive transmission for reliable power delivery. Metal construction assures long-lasting, stable operation.

A Powerful Force in Your Kitchen

The bowl-lift stand mixer is built with sturdy metal arms that raise and lower the bowl with an easy turn of the lift lever. This commercial-style mixer has the power, strength, and capacity to handle your toughest recipes. The PowerKnead™ Spiral Dough Hook, for example, replicates hand kneading with greater force.

The style ... is matched by the **power, strength, and capacity** to handle your toughest recipes.

bowl-lift stand mixers

Stir the Senses

The KitchenAid® hand mixer is convenient and durable, making it the perfect solution for the variety of foods you cook in the kitchen. Mix a batch of chocolate chip cookies in minutes or whip egg whites to make the perfect meringue. And, the hand mixer is the ideal complement to your KitchenAid® stand mixer. While the stand mixer is kneading bread dough, you can reach for the hand mixer and whip up a filling, topping, or flavored butter.

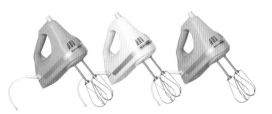

The KitchenAid® hand mixer is
"the total package ...
powerful, quiet, controlled."*

*National culinary testing publication

Cabinets and Hardware by KraftMaid®

Blending Beautiful Memories

Whether it's a conversation over fresh fruit smoothies or relaxing with creamy milkshakes, a KitchenAid® blender gives you the ability to turn any gathering into a cozy celebration. And it's not just about beverages. Your KitchenAid® blender is the ideal tool for preparing savory soups, spicy salsas, or perfect puréed sauces.

Your KitchenAid® blender is
the ideal tool ... providing
the right amount of power
for different applications.

Processing Your Day

Life can be hectic, whether it's getting the kids to school or rushing home from work to cook for the family. Let the KitchenAid® food processor help simplify your life. Reduce the need to stop and clean by choosing a model that offers multiple work bowls such as the Chef's Bowl, a Mini Bowl, or both.

Choose your ingredients
and prepare them
the way you want.

hand mixers, blenders, food processors

Cook for the Cure®

gives those with a **passion** for cooking a way to **support** Susan G. Komen for the Cure® and the **fight against** breast cancer.

COOK FOR THE CURE is a registered trademark of Susan G. Komen for the Cure.®

SUSAN G.
Komen
FOR THE
CURE

For additional information about KitchenAid® countertop appliances, visit KitchenAid.com or call the KitchenAid Customer Satisfaction Center at 800-541-6390. We'll help you select the ideal model, answer questions about appliance operation and performance, and give you a point of contact should you ever need service.

Our unique, hassle-free warranty is the most consumer-friendly in the industry. If any KitchenAid® PRO LINE® Series product fails within the first two years of ownership, or any other KitchenAid® product fails within the first year of ownership, KitchenAid will deliver a replacement free of charge. For complete warranty information, call the KitchenAid Customer Satisfaction Center at 800.541.6390, ask your dealer, or visit KITCHENAID.COM

KitchenAid®
FOR THE WAY IT'S MADE.®